The Godfather

Director
Francis Ford Coppola

Note by William Malyszko

 Longman

 York Press

York Press
322 Old Brompton Road, London SW5 9JH

Pearson Education Limited
Edinburgh Gate, Harlow, Essex CM20 2JE, United Kingdom
Associated companies, branches and representatives throughout
the world

First published 2001
Second impression 2002

ISBN 0-582-43188-3

Designed by Vicki Pacey
Phototypeset by Gem Graphics, Trenance, Mawgan Porth, Cornwall
Colour reproduction and film output by Spectrum Colour
Produced by Pearson Education North Asia Limited, Hong Kong

contents

To my wife, my parents and my
students, who all taught me more
than they realise.

author of this note   William Malyszko is the Head of
Media and Film Studies and Senior Teacher at Langley Park School for Boys
in Beckenham, Kent. He is a contributing author on film in *GCSE Media
Studies* (Longman) and an A Level Media Studies examiner.

background

trailer

Original reviews (1972) declare *The Godfather* a hit ...

... The year's first really satisfying, big commercial American film ... a movie that describes a sorrowful American Dream as a slam-bang, sentimental gangster drama.

One of the most brutal and moving chronicles of American life ever designed within the limits of popular entertainment.

An east-side audience last Friday night murmured with satisfaction every time an enemy of the family was dispatched. The slaughter was choreographed with such precision that one member of the audience was heard to sigh 'Beautiful!' at one particularly sanguine execution.

The New York Times

The Godfather is a movie that seems to have everything – warmth, violence, nostalgia, the charisma of Marlon Brando in one of his finest performances, and the dynastic sweep of an Italian-American *Gone With the Wind.*

Time

Francis Ford Coppola has stayed very close to the book's greased lightning sensationalism and yet has made a movie with the spaciousness and strength that popular novels such as Dickens used to have. The direction is tenaciously intelligent.

The New Yorker

An extraordinary achievement: a new classic in a classic American film genre. It will take some kind of movie to prevent *The Godfather* from dominating next year's Academy Awards. A product of almost limitless commercial potential.

The Washington Post

'totally without moral substance'

Or do they ...?

> But it is overlong at about 175 minutes (played without intermission), and occasionally confusing. While never so placid as to be boring, it is never so gripping as to be superior screen drama. This should not mar Paramount's box office expectations in any measure, though some filmgoers may be disappointed.
>
> *Variety*

> Al Pacino rattles around in a part too demanding for him. Brando's make-up is poor, the score by Nino Rota is surprisingly rotten, and the print had very washed out colors.
>
> *New Republic*

> The success of *The Godfather* is deplorable, if you believe that popular entertainment both reflects and modifies social morale. In a sentence, the picture forces you to take sides, to form allegiances, in a situation that is totally without moral substance.
>
> *The Nation*

> ... swelled into an overblown, pretentious, slow, and ultimately tedious three-hour quasi-epic.
>
> *Vogue*

> Far from surviving as the *Gone With the Wind* of gangster movies, my guess is that *The Godfather* will be as quickly forgotten as it deserves to be.
>
> *New York Post*

reading the godfather

Consider a film that had:

- ■ A penniless young director without a hit to his name
- ■ A has-been **star** who was at the time considered a loser
- ■ A young unknown lead that the studio did not want
- ■ An egotistical movie executive who fired the director three times
- ■ An initial budget of just $2 million, which ballooned to $6 million
- ■ An initial shoot of just 53 days

number one favourite film of all time

■ A studio ranked a poor ninth in the industry

■ An author who sold the rights to the studio for a mere $12,000

Then realise that this same film:

■ Won the Oscar for Best Picture

■ Won the Oscar for Best Actor and rejuvenated the star's career

■ Won the Oscar for Best Screenplay for the director/writer and instantly made him hot property

■ Led to a sequel that also won the Oscar for Best Picture (amongst others) – the only time that this has been achieved by a sequel

■ Made a star of the young lead who is still in the A list nearly 30 years later

■ Took $25 million in its first three weeks at the box office and $110 million on its first full release – beating the record set by *Gone With the Wind* in 1939

■ Sent the stock of the parent company to $44.75 per share in 1972, an all-time high

■ Was sold to NBC for the highest price ever for a single television showing of a film

■ Had initial and second-run box office sales that both broke industry records

■ Started a small industry of sequels, videos, television versions, books, etc.

■ Redefined its genre and brought it back from near extinction

■ Was voted the number one favourite film of all time in an Internet poll in the year 2000 – a position it has consistently maintained

That film was *The Godfather*.

It is proof, if proof were needed, that the screenwriter and guru William Goldman's maxim about Hollywood was absolutely true: 'Nobody knows anything.'

The most obvious aspect of *The Godfather* when first seeing it is that it is a gangster film – one of the great American genres. But at the time of

the great American dream was dead

production in the 1970s the gangster movie was at its lowest ebb; its popularity had fallen during the 1960s and few film-makers were interested in what seemed a tired genre. It suffered much the same fate as the western – out of touch with contemporary themes. In fact, a recent film, *The Brotherhood* (Martin Ritt, 1968), had made many people feel that, as successful as Mario Puzo's novel was, audiences were just not interested in the cheap and nasty lives of Mafia mobsters. This Kirk Douglas vehicle failed miserably at the box office and industry people shied away from the challenge of tackling this genre. Francis Ford Coppola changed all this.

The film has many notable features for its time:

■ It presented the central mob as a close-knit family

■ It made gangsters seem real – we watch them doing ordinary things and having the same feelings and emotions that we all have

■ The **narrative**, characterisation and performances are successful at making us see these people as tragic figures

■ It took its time – at well over two hours long, the majority of the film shows people sitting and talking

■ It is very dark – Coppola was determined to create a particular visual atmosphere, very much against the wishes of the studio

■ It prepared the way for franchises and blockbusters of the next thirty years

■ It was supposedly based on real events, such as Johnny Fontane being a thinly disguised Frank Sinatra

To understand this film fully we need to read it as a **text** of its time. It was produced during a period when Americans were quite critical of their leaders. The Vietnam War and the Nixon administration, which led to the Watergate scandal, had created considerable unrest. The central metaphor of the Mafia as representative of corporate America would not be lost on many members of the audience. They would also have recognised the brave message that the great American dream was dead.

It is a film that is set in the second half of the 1940s but has a distinct 1970s sensibility in its **style**. The world of these gangsters is filmed in quite a glamorous way and this aspect of their depiction upset some members of the public at the time.

The violence in the film, although tame by today's standards, also created an uproar in the press. It raised many questions relating to the declining values and morality of Hollywood.

The general public, however, gave an answer to the chattering classes that was irrefutable. *The Godfather* was one of the most popular and profitable films of all time and was a sensation in cinemas throughout the United States and the world.

More important is its contribution to both the genre and film in general. Almost every major gangster film made since 1972 has owed this one an immense debt.

key players' biographies

FRANCIS FORD COPPOLA – DIRECTOR

Francis Ford Coppola has been referred to as the leading member of the Brat Pack of young American directors of the 1970s. These tyros were educated film-makers who rejected the idea that they had to serve a long apprenticeship in the industry. They felt that they already possessed the talent, imagination and skills required to make great films. His fellow 'brats' were people such as George Lucas, Steven Spielberg, Peter Bogdanovich and Martin Scorsese.

Coppola was born in Detroit, Michigan, in 1939 and graduated from UCLA film school before becoming a jack-of-all-trades for Roger Corman, the horror-schlockmeister probably best known for his Edgar Allan Poe adaptations. Coppola's time with Corman culminated in a director/writer credit for *Dementia 13* (Francis Ford Coppola, 1963), a film about an axe-murderer, which he shot in just two weeks, but an argument between the two over the first cut soon resulted in a brief falling out. (Coppola, incidentally, gave Corman a part in *The Godfather Part II*.) Even at the beginning Coppola was prepared to speak his mind and to take on his superiors, much as he did during the making of *The Godfather*.

This experience, however, led to a few writing jobs, such as *This Property is*

biographies

biographies

biographies

biographies

biographies

biographies

biographies

biographies

biographies

biographies

confidence to take on the impossible

Condemned (Sydney Pollack, 1966), for which Coppola received a screen credit, and *Reflections in a Golden Eye* (John Huston, 1967), for which Coppola's screenplay was in fact rejected. Being an ambitious young man, Coppola was keen to develop his own projects so he bought the rights to a rites-of-passage book entitled *You're a Big Boy Now* (film, 1966). He directed this using new high-speed film so that he could shoot at night and on location in New York – an experience that was invaluable for the future director of *The Godfather*.

His first major break, however, came with the film *Finian's Rainbow* (1968), a 1940s-style musical starring Fred Astaire. With typical Coppola ego he fired the choreographer and decided to stage the numbers himself, as well as appoint his father, Carmine, as the musical director. The film contains an excess of very flashy camerawork to cover up for the fact that the director actually knew little about dancing. The hallmarks of Coppola's approach were becoming clear by this stage: confidence to take on the impossible and to have no compunction about using members of his family in his films. In *The Godfather* Carmine Coppola composed some of the music for the wedding and Coppola's sister, Talia Shire, played the role of Connie Corleone. Later in the series Coppola bravely cast his daughter, Sofia, as Michael Corleone's daughter in *The Godfather Part III* and his father's dominance in the music department grew with each film in the trilogy. He also cast his nephew, Nicolas Cage, in *Peggy Sue Got Married* (Francis Coppola, 1986).

Coppola had made only four feature films prior to *The Godfather*, all of which failed at the box office. Coppola was a man of huge ambition. He created his own film studio, American Zoetrope, so that he could be free from the artistic constraints of the majors. Unfortunately, by 1971 he was in immense debt to Warner Brothers and the dream seemed destined to remain just that.

One of Coppola's main talents was in screenwriting. He had just written the screenplay for a film called *Patton* – a vehicle for George C. Scott in 1969. It went on to win Coppola an Oscar for best screenplay during the shooting of *The Godfather* in 1971.

Paramount took a big risk in giving the film *The Godfather* to Coppola in the first place. He seemed to be the director by default – they couldn't find anyone else and they appeared set on giving it to an Italian to deflect any criticism voiced by the Italian-American Civil Rights League. The gamble paid off. Coppola won the Oscar for Best Adapted Screenplay (with Mario Puzo), which he also won two years later with *The Godfather Part II* – for which he also won Best Director and the film itself won Best Picture.

The success of *The Godfather* made Coppola a millionaire and the temporary wealth enabled him to pay off his debts to Warner Brothers. He could now concentrate on creating the American Zoetrope that he wanted and embarked on a very personal project, *The Conversation* (1974), a film inspired to some degree by Michelangelo Antonioni's *Blow-Up* (1966). Coppola was clearly setting out his stall – he saw himself as an auteur – a maker of art – a rejection of the Hollywood hegemony and an embracing of the European tradition. After all, he was an Italian, a European, albeit an American one.

The Conversation was a critical success, but not particularly successful at the box office. It led Coppola to return to *The Godfather* franchise – something he would do again when he was in financial trouble at the end of the 1980s and decided to direct the third part of the trilogy.

Following this, he embarked on his most daunting and personal film yet: *Apocalypse Now* (1979). This was a four-year project, which in many ways took Coppola to the brink. It put a strain on his marriage, his finances, his health, his career. But it paid off – it was very well received and reinforced his standing as a major director and artist and, to this day, is considered by many to be a classic and certainly one of the best films made about America's involvement in Vietnam.

Over the next twenty years this pattern repeated itself. Coppola veers from very personal films, such as *One from the Heart* (1982) to mainstream Hollywood fare, such as *Bram Stoker's Dracula* (1992). American Zoetrope has been a huge drain on his resources and demonstrated many of the problems of independence in a Hollywood-dominated industry.

The industry still hears rumours that *The Godfather Part IV* is in his mind, but only time will tell. Will he be lured back to the saga to continue a work of art – or will he simply need the money?

biographies

MARLON BRANDO – ACTOR

Marlon Brando is one of the most important figures in American film acting of the last half-century. He is a leading player, some would say the father of, the American interpretation of the Stanislavsky school of acting, referred to as **Method acting**.

The most important influence on Brando's early career was Stella Adler, one of the original members of the Group Theatre, founded by Harold Clurman (later to be her husband) and Lee Strasberg (who, incidentally, plays an important role in *The Godfather Part II*). This theatre used the ideas developed by Stanislavsky at the beginning of the twentieth century, which stressed the need for the actor to delve deeply into his or her emotional experience in preparation for a part. The foundation of the Group Theatre involved a moral, intellectual and professional discourse to do with acting in its widest sense.

Adler's concepts relied on the use of detailed observation by the actor in order to inform the role and create a realistic performance. When she met Brando she felt that this 'puppy' (her word) was an ideal pupil for this new and vibrant approach to acting. Her teachings moulded the embryonic star.

The early successes for Brando in cinema were *A Streetcar Named Desire* (Elia Kazan, 1951), for which the actor received an Oscar nomination, the iconic *The Wild One* (Laslo Benedek, 1952) and *On the Waterfront* (Elia Kazan, 1954), for which Brando won the Oscar for Best Actor. Brando's early work with Kazan was no accident – the director was himself an advocate of the Method and deeply influenced by Strasberg, so the pairing was not only obvious, but also very creative.

The distinct persona that Brando brought to his performances was that of the young rebel out to wreak revenge on the world, a persona that was to influence the young James Dean, amongst others. In *The Wild One*, in response to the question, 'What are you rebelling against?' Brando replies, 'What've you got?'

Brando's style, however, was not admired by all – some found the mumbling, the glances off-camera, the business with his hands or body, very irritating. It was a style that some felt was too mannered; others

the actor's ability to use improvisation

considered it a breath of fresh air as the performances frequently relied on intense yet convincing emotions and an aesthetic that portrayed realism at its best. It fitted well with the themes and narratives of these new directors and their socially conscious movies. Look closely at the opening scene of *The Godfather* and observe how Brando's voice and mannerisms add to the part – such as when he smells the flower in his lapel as he speaks of murder, as if to take away the smell of the blood.

An integral part of the teaching of the Method was the actor's ability to use improvisation to search for the truth within the character. Scenes such as the one between Brando and Rod Steiger, a fellow Method actor, in the back of the car in *On the Waterfront*, where Brando gives his now famous speech 'I could have been a contender', are renowned for the actor actually changing or adding to the script during the shooting of the film. Or the scene with Brando and Eva Marie Saint in the park in the same film, when Brando picks up the glove she has dropped and starts playing with it as he talks to her about what she wants – the glove acting metonymically as her, telling us what *he* wants, which is to hold and cherish her, as he does the glove. In *The Godfather*, for example, the scene of the death of Don Corleone was improvised from an idea Brando had on the set, based on real-life experiences with his own children.

Throughout the 1950s and '60s Brando made a number of interesting films, such as *Guys and Dolls* (Joseph Mankiewicz, 1955), *The Young Lions* (Edward Dmytryk, 1958) and *Mutiny on the Bounty* (Lewis Milestone, 1962), but his choices were often so varied and idiosyncratic that many of his films were box-office flops. By the time of the casting of *The Godfather* in 1971 many felt that his days as a major Hollywood star were over.

At one point, during the making of *The Godfather*, he threatened to leave the production when Evans fired Coppola. The director was reinstated, and the rest is history.

After *The Godfather* Brando made, amongst other films, the notorious *Last Tango in Paris* (Bernardo Bertolucci, 1972) and *Apocalypse Now* (Francis Ford Coppola, 1979), and was cast as the eponymous hero's father in *Superman* (Richard Donner, 1978) for a multimillion dollar fee for a few minutes of acting. He sent up his own performance in *The Godfather* by cheekily recreating the Don's persona in *The Freshman* (Andrew Bergman, 1990).

Paradoxically, Brando has scorned his profession in numerous interviews. He sees writers as varied as Shakespeare and Tennessee Williams as true artists and the actors as merely tools. When he won the Oscar for Best Performance in *The Godfather* he sent along to the ceremony a Native American called Satcheen Littlefeather to refuse the prize and to publicise the plight of her race. He finds actors' awards a superficial aspect of the business and, being the intellectual he is, rejects the glitter that is not gold.

AL PACINO – ACTOR

In 1966, a young out-of-work and penniless actor, Al Pacino joined the Actors' Studio in New York, run by the acting guru Lee Strasberg. This made him ideal casting opposite Brando. To Pacino, Brando was a legend. Himself trained in Method acting, Pacino was given the opportunity to work with the master when he was cast in *The Godfather*.

Pacino had won awards for his work on the New York stage, but up to this point he had appeared in only two films – *Me, Natalie* (Fred Coe, 1969) and *The Panic in Needle Park* (Jerry Schatzberg, 1971) – both minor, although the latter did attract some attention at Cannes. The studio was very reluctant to cast Pacino, considering him funny-looking and unattractive. Coppola insisted, convinced that he had the right man for Michael, as was the co-star Robert Duvall.

The success of *The Godfather* rocketed Pacino to the star status that he retains to this day, despite some low moments such as his starring role in the box-office disaster *Revolution* (Hugh Hudson, 1985). Pacino has received seven Oscar nominations (including one for his performance in *The Godfather*) and finally won the coveted prize for his performance in *Scent of a Woman* (Martin Brest, 1992) in which he played a blind ex-soldier who teaches a young student (Chris O'Donnell) about the joys of life.

Pacino's other notable films include: *Serpico* (Sidney Lumet, 1973); *Dog*

the story of a family of murderers

Day Afternoon (Sidney Lumet, 1975); *Scarface* (Brian De Palma, 1983); *Sea of Love* (Harold Becker, 1989); *Frankie & Johnny* (Garry Marshall, 1991); *Carlito's Way* (Brian De Palma, 1993); *Heat* (Michael Mann, 1995); *Donnie Brasco* (Mike Newell, 1997).

Not bad for a man who also turned down leading roles in *Star Wars* (George Lucas, 1977); *Kramer vs Kramer* (Robert Benton, 1979); *Apocalypse Now* (Francis Ford Coppola, 1979); *Born on the Fourth of July* (Oliver Stone, 1989); *Pretty Woman* (Garry Marshall, 1990) and *Crimson Tide* (Tony Scott, 1995).

Pacino has been going through a prolific period at the turn of the millennium, including *Chinese Coffee* (2000), in which he stars, but which is also his feature-film directorial debut, although he did previously direct an interesting documentary called *Looking for Richard* (1996), an examination of the actor's preparation for the role of Richard III. Pacino, like Coppola, sees his work as serious and important. He frequently chooses films that are controversial in their subject matter, such as the recently made *The Insider* (Michael Mann, 1999) and *Any Given Sunday* (Oliver Stone, 1999).

In polls of great actors of all time, Al Pacino is usually in the top ten, if not top five.

MARIO PUZO – WRITER

Mario Puzo was born in New York in 1920 and through a tough, unromantic working-class upbringing rejected the notion of the stereotype of happy, singing Italians. Instead, he found the story of a family of murderers a more inspiring, and realistic, portrayal of Italian life.

His first two novels, *Dark Arena* (1953) and *Fortunate Pilgrim* (1964) were very well received but barely earned him a living. When the publishing house suggested that he needed more of the Mafia in his books, *The Godfather* was born. He was forty-five years of age and in immense debt so anything that looked as though it might become a blockbuster was worthy of his attention. Ultimately the paperback rights for the publication of the book were sold for $410,000 – a record at the time – and the book was a huge success.

biographies background

two rather large egos

The importance of Puzo in the *Godfather* trilogy is threefold: first, he was an Italian, and this helped both in merchandising the product and in placating some members of the Italian-American Civil Rights League. Second, he created a basic story and characters that were the foundation for the tragedy that Coppola saw in the book. Third, Puzo and Coppola had a very creative working relationship in all three screenplays. It will be interesting to see if Coppola could return to the franchise without Puzo, who died in 1999.

ROBERT EVANS – STUDIO EXECUTIVE

Evans, a former matinée idol and Hollwood playboy, was controversially appointed the Head of Productions at Paramount Studios in 1970 – he held the important position of the person who can give a green light to a project. One of the first things he did was to acquire new property for the studio, including *Love Story* by Erich Segal (1970; film, 1970). His wife, Ali MacGraw, was cast in the leading female role and the film went on to receive six Oscar nominations and earn a bucket-load of money. Evans had proven himself at the age of forty, within a year of being in the post.

One of Evans's next properties was *The Godfather*, for which he bought the film option for a mere $12,000 and $85,000 if they made the film – a pittance in relation to the ultimate rewards of the franchise for the studio. Later on, a more lucrative fee was offered to Mario Puzo to write the screenplay.

Stories abound concerning the difficult relationship between Evans and Coppola. One example concerns the final cut of the film. Evans claims he had a considerable hand in this, but Coppola maintains that the final cut was his. The problem lay in the two rather large egos, which collided during the shooting of the film: Coppola the poor creative artist, Evans the millionaire playboy.

Evans went on to produce some notable films, and others not so notable, for example: *Chinatown* (Roman Polanski, 1974), *Marathon Man* (John Schlesinger, 1976), *Popeye* (Robert Altman, 1980), *The Cotton Club* (Francis Coppola, 1984), *Sliver* (Phillip Noyce, 1993).

THE GODFATHER

a consistency of style and themes

ALBERT S. RUDDY – PRODUCER

Al Ruddy was best known in the 1960s as the co-creator of a popular television series called *Hogan's Heroes*. He has produced a huge number of lesser known and minor films such as *The Cannonball Run* (1980) and in recent years has predominantly worked in television.

Without doubt his major achievement as a producer was *The Godfather*. How much credit for the final film can go to Ruddy is debatable, but it is certain that he was useful in dealing with Evans and Coppola and their mercurial relationship.

director as auteur

Although the idea of a film text having an 'author', much like a novelist or playwright, has been around since 1913 in German writings, the full impact of the concept was not really considered until more recently. Auteur theory was proposed by the critics of the influential French magazine of the 1950s, *Cahiers du cinéma*, under the editorship of André Bazin. Many of these critics themselves subsequently became film-makers of the French New Wave in the 1960s: Jean-Luc Godard, François Truffaut, Jacques Rivette, Eric Rohmer, Claude Chabrol. In the 1960s in America the critic Andrew Sarris developed and popularised many of these critics' ideas.

The 'auteur' view of film-making proposes that the director can be seen as the author of the text. It is he or she who determines most, if not all, of the essential elements of the construction of a text in the minds of the audience and who gives it its identity while applying his or her personal vision. A consistency of style and themes is evident across the series of an auteur's films. Examples of directors whom the *Cahiers* critics championed as auteurs were Alfred Hitchcock, Howard Hawks, Nicholas Ray, Roberto Rossellini, Jean Renoir and Robert Bresson.

The critique around the auteur theory includes the following:

■ If a film is a work of art, who is the artist?

■ The characteristics of a director's individuality can be evident

■ Style is as important as the narrative itself – technique is as important as content

director as auteur

■ A director controls more creative aspects of a production than any other person involved

■ Hollywood films are worthy of study if we can talk of authorship in this way

■ Detailed analysis reveals the creative force of the auteur

■ The director's signature can function in much the same way as a star's presence

■ The director's ideology will pervade all aspects of the creative functions

■ Auteur theory provides another method of analysis and elevates the study of film

The theory has been much debated, and many critics argue that most film directors are not truly the author of their texts because film is a cooperative effort and numerous experts provide a specialist input to this collaborative art form. The cast and crew list of any film demonstrates the vast numbers of people involved. Some argue that many directors are merely metteurs-en-scène, in other words they simply bring other people's ideas together with little original input themselves.

The Godfather is a case in point. It had a wide variety of talented people working on the project, such as Gordon Willis as cinematographer, Dean Tavoularis as production designer, Anne Hill Johnson as costume designer, Nino Rota as composer, not to mention the wealth of talent in the acting ranks.

Alfred Hitchcock was vigorously championed by the *Cahiers* critics as a leading example of the auteur theory. Yet he argued himself that the two most creative aspects of making a film were the pre-production development and writing of the script and the post-production editing of the film – in some films these are both areas where the director may have limited involvement. In the case of *The Godfather* it is well documented that Coppola had a huge input in all areas of production: screenplay, principal photography and the final cut. In subsequent films in the trilogy he was also the producer.

There is further evidence of Coppola as an auteur on *The Godfather*. The first aspect of this is that he transformed a novel that was a simplistic

the film was Coppola's vision

potboiler into a subtle and dramatic piece of cinema. Coppola had a very good eye and ear for the distinct language of film and would brutally excise anything that did not serve the story in cinematic terms. The original novelist and co-scriptwriter, Mario Puzo, did not have the experience or skill that Coppola had gained on his previous works. The film was Coppola's vision, as the novel was Puzo's.

It is also clear in the production history of the film that Coppola was the driving force behind the vision:

■ He insisted on the casting of Brando and Pacino

■ He insisted on filming many scenes in New York and on real locations, rather than simply using a studio lot

■ He changed the **plot** to highlight the unique selling point of the narrative, the importance of the family, and thereby made these monsters seem human

■ He created a distinct technique and style for the **genre**, frequently resulting in titanic arguments with the director of photography – for example, Coppola insisted on low lighting to create dark scenes such as the film's opening scene

■ He was keen to use the imaginative input of actors during principal photography. He allowed them to improvise scenes before shooting – for example, the death of Don Corleone was an idea of Brando's and improvised with a scared little boy

■ He did not consider the shooting script to be sacrosanct – he would make instant decisions on the set if he came up with a better idea

■ He fought the studio's creative constraints and his determined temperament meant that he usually won – or was fired (three times)

But perhaps the most convincing argument is that Coppola created an **epic** within this almost extinct genre: it spreads over three generations and took twenty years to complete. Although Puzo wrote the original novel, Coppola created many artistic aspects of the whole trilogy and fought to retain his artistic control. He made the team see his vision, so clear in much of the documentary footage of the making of the films. In fact, the documentary

auteur qualities are evident in his oeuvre

Hearts of Darkness: a Filmmaker's Apocalypse (Fax Bahr, George Hickenlooper, 1991; partly filmed by Eleanor Coppola, his wife) shows in detail the struggle of the same auteur to bring a mammoth vision to life, only a few years after *The Godfather*, when he made *Apocalypse Now*.

Ideological aspects are also important in recognising an auteur. The central conceit of the family was instantly attractive to the director. He shares Puzo's paradoxical view that the family was the most important aspect of these people's lives, yet that the very structure of this patriarchy is the one thing that leads to their spiritual emptiness.

Outside this film, it can be seen that auteur qualities are evident in his oeuvre as a whole, which is marked by:

- recurring themes of familial breakdown or failure
- definitions of identity and cultural roots
- preoccupations with patriarchal figures
- a constant desire to reveal hypocrisy
- recurring Catholicism: sin, guilt, redemption, confession, punishment
- myths, dreams, fantasies

In addition to this there is Coppola's style. He is inclined towards very operatic and expressionist scenes or moments in his films. We can see this in works such as *Bram Stoker's Dracula*, where the Gothic sensibility and romantic aesthetic combined to create a sense of tragedy and pathos of much larger proportions than in the original work. From the grandeur of the Oscar-winning costume design by Eiko Ishioka, to the excesses of the acting by Gary Oldman and Anthony Hopkins and a narrative that turns one of the most evil creations in literature into a sympathetic and noble hero, we can see Coppola's fingerprints.

If we turn to the trilogy itself, we can see this style grow in stature as Coppola finishes *The Godfather Part III* inside and outside an opera house as we listen to the moving strains of Pietro Mascagni's *Cavalleria Rusticana*. As the family grows in both power and corruption, Coppola applies equally forceful visual and aural signifiers, combined with a

Coppola did write the screenplay

hyperbolic image of the Mafia don as cathartic, hubristic and ultimately lonely hero.

But perhaps the overwhelming argument in favour of Coppola as auteur lies in the original conception of auteur theory. If the *Cahiers* critics were rejecting the pre-eminence of the writer in this art form, the argument against them is just that: the writer who creates the scenes in the first place is really the omnipotent artist. And, of course, Coppola did write the screenplay.

narrative & form

theme

Themes in a film are used in a number of different ways. They can be:

- A structuring device to help with the **narrative**
- A character **motif**
- An **ideological** standpoint
- A signifier of **genre**
- A **style**
- A concept
- The controlling idea – what the film is really about
- A mood that pervades the film
- A message or moral

Because themes are woven into the fabric of the film in various ways, they are best discussed in context. We have already touched on themes in the previous section on auteurism. In later sections of this Note we will look also at themes in three major areas: Narrative, Style and Ideology.

narrative

Film narrative is the telling of a story through sounds, **dialogue**, music and imagery. This simple statement, however, belies the complexity of the narrative structure of most films, especially in something as dense as *The Godfather*. There are many different ways of approaching the study of narrative, each with its own particular emphasis or difference, and often with overlapping areas of agreement between different approaches.

THE GODFATHER

'a romance about a king with three sons'

It is inevitable in this section that we must also touch upon character as the two concepts are interdependent. In a later section we will look at character analysis in a little more detail (see Character).

CLASSICAL TRAGEDY: ARISTOTLE

Aristotle (384–322BC) presented a theory of narrative in relation to near contemporary tragedies, such as those by Sophocles (495–406BC). His work has been influential ever since, especially to one of our major dramatists, William Shakespeare (1564–1616). His ideas can be applied to the structure of *The Godfather* in many ways, particularly as one of the major themes of the film is its mythic and tragic nature.

Coppola saw *The Godfather* as 'a romance about a king with three sons', resonating with reference to *King Lear*, one of Shakespeare's major tragedies. The success of this film is partly due to the stature of this ambition – to make a film about a family of gangsters, make them sympathetic to the audience and draw parallels with contemporary society.

A tragedy is basically a story with a serious theme that usually ends in the death of a leading character. A tragedy needs certain qualities, according to Aristotle, to work its magic upon an audience. Although this can become quite complicated when studying a great tragedy such as *Hamlet*, some of the more significant aspects of this theory can be relatively simply put. Over the centuries other critics have adapted these ideas and added to them and later we will particularly look at the work of a Hollywood script-doctor and guru, Robert McKee.

■ **protagonist hero** The **protagonist** is the leading character – the one the tragedy centres on. The essential ingredient here is that our **hero** could have been a great king. Michael has qualities that would make him a great leader in the non-criminal world. He is a war hero. He is loyal. He is, at the start of the film, morally upright. He wants to do the right thing.

■ **hamartia**, the error of judgement or the tragic flaw. The hero makes a major mistake because of the flaw in his nature. Michael's love and his loyalty for his father set him on a morally self-destructive course: from

The audience literally cry

the moment he tells his father he will take care of him, Michael's future is set.

■ **climax and crisis** A dramatic high point that leads to the turning point in the story: from this point on our hero cannot return to the stability he once enjoyed – he inevitably moves towards the catastrophe (the end result) that he has created. Once Michael has killed Sollozzo and McCluskey he is part of the brotherhood – he has 'made his bones', as the Mafia would say.

■ **hubris** Pride or overweening confidence that makes the protagonist ignore the right moral path. The hero cannot see his own flaw, no matter how perceptive he may be about other people's weaknesses. Michael's love for his father, and then the family, corrupts his initially moral vision. In Michael's case it is unthinkable to him that he will not vanquish his enemies.

■ **retribution** Our hero must be seen to suffer for his sins – in classical tragedy he must ultimately die at the moment he has the full realisation of what he has done. In Michael's case it is a much more modern slant: he lives to watch the suffering of those closest to him.

■ **catharsis** The audience find that their emotions cleanse their own soul – 'There, but for the grace of God, go I.' We may recognise aspects of ourselves in the hero, including his flaw. The audience literally cry with the pain. This link was not lost on Aristotle. The emotional experience makes you feel better – you have not made these mistakes and thrown away everything you prize, including your soul. This is an important aspect and modern commentators on film have stressed the importance of examining the relationship between the text and the audience, or, perhaps more accurately, the spectacle and the spectator. The feelings of tragic loss in a text are also referred to as pathos.

Aristotle's ideas give us one way into understanding the structure of a narrative as a whole. These ideas have been adapted by film-makers and critics of the last century in many different ways. For example, Aristotle was interested in our human understanding of fate and the individual facing up to the moral choices available to him or her. In more recent times our discourse has embraced existentialism – the individual

Michael can be seen as an existential hero

being intensely aware of his or her own existence, freedom and accompanying responsibilities. Michael can be seen as an existential hero, not just a tragic one. The film creates a vision of the embryonic Michael of *Parts II and III*, one who is alone and lonely. Coppola increasingly inserts shots of Michael alone, sitting, thinking, and this image grows throughout the trilogy:

> Uneasy lies the head that wears a crown.
>
> *King Henry VI, Part 2*

Michael is left with the one thing he cannot destroy: his guilt. So, unlike the tragic heroes of Sophocles or Shakespeare, he does not die. He lives with the responsibility that he has created – he watches others die, including his family – a fate worse than death itself.

From these points it is clear that narrative and character are inextricably linked and our understanding of the narrative is dependent upon what the characters do – especially in such a visual form as film. Action *is* character.

THE THREE-ACT STRUCTURE

Classical Hollywood style texts have generally adopted the three-Act structure. *The Godfather* breaks down into three Acts as follows:

Act I

Introduction:
The wedding sequence and Don Corleone in his study
The Hollywood sequence when Tom Hagen meets Woltz
Complication:
The Sollozzo business
First Act climax:
The hit on Don Corleone (0.43.49)

Act II

Sollozzo and Tom
Sonny's leadership and revenge
The hospital scene

essentially a plot in three acts

The mid-Act climax – the turning point:
The murder of Sollozzo
The Sicily sequence
The murder of Sonny
End-of-Act climax:
The murder of Appolonia (2.00.49)

Act III
Don Corleone calls a meeting of the five families
Michael returns
Michael takes over the business
Don Corleone dies
The climax of the film – dénouement:
Michael exacts revenge
Closure:
Michael becomes the new Don (2.45.25)

The Godfather is essentially a plot in three acts, in much the same way that Shakespeare's plays are plotted in five Acts.

The first Act of *The Godfather* presents us with the world of the characters as it exists at a particular time: it is a relatively stable world as far as the audience can tell, as it represents a habitual ebb and flow of family and business events. Once Coppola has established the characters and the set-up, the narrative can then be given a complication – the introduction of the essential aspect of conflict that drives the narrative. But this complication can occur only once we have understood this initially stable situation, as all narratives, and characters within them, involve change effected by conflict.

In *The Godfather*, complication is caused by the introduction of the following conflicts:

■ Sollozzo wants to set up business in narcotics with the help of the Don
■ Don Corleone has objections to this particular kind of crime
■ The other dons disagree. Result: war

RITES OF PASSAGE AS STRUCTURE

The first sequence of the film is set during a wedding reception. Coppola uses all of the rites of passage (baptism, marriage, funeral) in this film for a number of reasons. For example:

■ They convey the community very clearly to the audience: we can quickly grasp, for example, the importance of the family, the wealth and power of the Don, the relationships between individual characters

■ Each rite creates a distinct atmosphere and mood: weddings, funerals and baptisms have particular associations for the audience, which Coppola can reinforce or subvert – he can use them to violate our expectation of what is going to happen

■ They are very visual – the mise-en-scène can reveal many aspects about this community

■ They involve spectacle – they please and entertain the audience

■ They all involve the family – they are central to the major themes

■ They are strong, economic, narrative devices, affording the meeting of many characters and narrative strands in one sequence

A wedding, of course, has specific connotations for the audience: it is a joyous affair – one that celebrates love, the creation of a family, the love of God. It is an ideal way of creating an atmosphere that is at odds with the parallel scenes of the Don executing his power – decisions that will result in other people's suffering and loss of life.

Weddings also identify character and familial relationships very quickly. For example, the Don refuses to have the family photograph taken without Michael present. When he does arrive, Michael insists that Kay – an outsider, a non-Italian, a WASP (white, anglo-saxon protestant) – be in the photograph. Michael is a war hero who wants nothing to do with the family business. His older brother Sonny is a hot-headed individual who indulges in illicit sexual relations with a maid of honour. Tom Hagen is the calm and loyal *consiglieri* who organises the business affairs. Fredo, the eldest Corleone brother, is drunk and weak. The mother has nothing to do with business, but is the emotional centre of the family.

already the king is disempowered

By the end of this sequence the following aspects of the narrative have been established:

■ the sub-plot concerning Johnny Fontane and the film producer Woltz
■ the sub-plot concerning Sollozzo
■ the reason for the next sequence – Tom is going to Los Angeles to see Woltz
■ the distance between Don Corleone and the other dons
■ that Bonasera owes the Don a favour
■ that Luca Brasi is a loyal strong-arm of the Don
■ that Sonny is adulterous, a potential weakness

By the time we end the first Act we have seen forty-four minutes of film and the following has already happened:

■ Tom Hagen has shown the real power, and violence, of the Don in his visit to Hollywood to persuade Woltz to give Johnny Fontane the part in the film. The infamous horse's head sequence has shocked the audience in spectacular fashion
■ The real villain, Sollozzo, has made his appearance and has complicated the relatively stable situation we started with. He has forced Don Corleone to make a decision that ultimately leads to war between mob members
■ The apparent leading character, the Don, has suffered an assassination attempt on his life

We have another two hours of viewing to go and already the king is disempowered.

The breakdown of the scenes into Acts, above, gives a guide to the examination of these ideas which space does not allow us to expand upon in the present volume.

HOLLYWOOD NARRATIVE STRUCTURE: McKEE

The American screenwriting guru and script-doctor, Robert McKee, gives an outline of the ideas of Aristotle, among others, as applied to Hollywood

McKee applies the rules learnt from Aristotle

films. He sees the modern three-Act structure as a variation of the five stages we may see in a classical play:

1. The inciting incident
2. Progressive complications
3. Crisis
4. Climax
5. Resolution

McKee applies the rules learnt from Aristotle and puts them into the context of Hollywood films. Applied to *The Godfather* they are as follows:

1. **The inciting incident** This radically upsets the balance of forces in the protagonist's life. An attempt is made on the Don's life

2. **Progressive complications** These lead to the ultimate high point of the story and force the protagonist to act. Sonny is assassinated. Michael takes a wife who is also assassinated. The Don dies. Michael is the new leading character

3. **Crisis** The protagonist makes a decision to act. Michael has two major moments in the film: he decides to kill Sollozzo and McCluskey; he decides to be the new godfather, taking on the burden that this role entails. The first crisis we may be sympathetic to, as he is merely killing murderers who wanted to kill his father. But the second one is more complex: his decision to take over the family business is a complete rejection of the moral values by which Michael had previously lived his life. He has now sold his soul to the Devil

4. **Climax** This is the major change in the character – a value swing from the positive to the negative – a highly dramatic example of how far the narrative has taken the hero. The baptism scene towards the end of the film shows how powerful Michael is and how destructive he can be

5. **Resolution** The new stability is now established. Michael is the Don – the other gangsters come to his study and pay homage to him as they did to his father. This involves a rejection of his wife, the one who is still morally upright.

NARRATIVE, STORY AND PLOT

These terms are often used loosely and interchangeably but they do have precise and different meanings that highlight the relationship between text and spectator. David Bordwell and Kristin Thompson in *Film Art – an Introduction* offer very useful distinctions here.

> **Narrative**: a chain of events in cause-effect relationships occurring in time and space.
>
> **Story**: all the events that we see and hear, as well as those that we infer or assume to have occurred, including their presumed causal relationships, chronological order, duration, frequence and spatial locations. Opposed to *plot*, which is the film's actual presentation of certain events in the narrative.
>
> **Plot**: all the events that are directly presented to us, including their causal relations, order, duration, frequency and spatial locations. Opposed to *story*, which is the viewer's imaginary construction of all events in the narrative.

Film-makers control what we see and hear and the order in which we see and hear it. Our minds rush to make cause (e.g., why did that happen?) and effect (e.g., what will happen next?) relations between events in our daily lives as it is a fundamental way that we understand the world. So it is with film narratives.

Coppola and Puzo create the plot that we see on the screen, but we, the audience, must recreate the story-text in our own minds as we do not necessarily see every event, but we do understand why or how it happened. For example, when we hear that Fredo is being sent to Las Vegas to learn the casino business we do not actually see him pack his bags, get on an aeroplane, arrive in Las Vegas, meet Moe Green, etc. It is not necessary for the plot, but we know that it must have happened as it is referred to in the Don's bedroom and later on we see the end result. If Fredo were the protagonist, however, we might well see all these scenes as they would give us an insight into his character and life.

the story is conditioned by the way the plot is delivered

SCHEMATA AND CULTURAL CAPITAL

Bordwell and Thompson also offer the term schemata – the precise mental models we have that enable us to read a film. For example, our understanding of *The Godfather* is partly dependent upon our past experience of the genre. So our mental models come from all sorts of places: viewing media texts; reading literature, magazines, newspapers; life experiences; education; nationality and race; upbringing and social class; gender; age. To put it bluntly, a fifty-year-old Sicilian American of 1972 is likely to read the film differently from an eighteen-year-old English film studies student in 2001.

The concept of cultural capital, coined by Pierre Bourdieu, is applicable here in helping us to understand how narratives work. This concept concerns the unequal distribution of cultural practices, values and competences within society. A simple way of looking at it is the difference between individuals and their cultural knowledge, and how some viewers may be less able fully to understand the complexity of a text because they cannot grasp the frames of reference within a text. Allusions and intertextual references depend on the original knowledge that the film-makers and the audience share.

It is hardly surprising, considering these ideas, that different people have widely alternative readings of, and reactions to, individual films and genres.

PARALLEL NARRATIVE

If we consider parallel narrative techniques we can also see the difference between plot and story.

In *The Godfather* parallel narrative is used in the dénouement of the last Act. The plot interweaves actions between one central scene, in the church, and five other locations: the barber shop, the hotel room, the courthouse, the lift, the revolving doors. If they were all shown one after another, after the entire baptism sequence, we would have a different sequence and a different effect. The story we are creating is conditioned by the way the plot is delivered. Again, we consider narrative and style together, as they are both powerful structural tools used in the creation of film.

Coppola finishes the film in bravura style

Coppola uses the baptism of Connie's son and the acceptance of Michael Corleone as the godfather as an ironic counterpoint to the numerous murders taking place contemporaneously at Michael's behest. Clearly many other meanings are being created by the use of this technique. So although the spectators are seeing a plot that is two parallel narratives interwoven, they are also making sense of the different locations and possibly time sequences because of what they have already learned in the film. The audience constructs the story.

The dénouement of a narrative of this kind is always important and often difficult. The text must offer a completion that satisfies, that is whole. The emotions of the audience have been manipulated by the storyteller, and if they feel cheated by the film's closure, then the spell is broken. Many potentially great films have been demolished by a weak ending.

Coppola finishes the film in bravura style: he takes an immense gamble in playing off the solemnity of the baptism of a child in a Roman Catholic church with the graphic slaughter of Michael's opponents. But this creates the perfect shock effect before the quiet but devastating ending. It is the ability of film to show us such contrasts that gives the medium its power.

The style of the parallel narrative depends upon using different techniques, for example:

■ cross-cutting between similar and contradictory shots

■ a variety of shots being used from extreme long shot to close-up (CU), from low angle to high angle

■ the use of different diegetic sounds, from those of the Latin spoken by the priest and the organ music in the baptism to those of the slaughter, a hail of automatic machine-gun fire and broken glass

■ the use of non-diegetic sounds – overlapping the baptism oration with the build-up and the executions, so they become non-diegetic in particular parts

■ the contradictory ambiences in each scene

■ the pace of the sequence as the baptism progresses and the climax of the assassinations take place

■ the ironic meanings created by the words and the actions

a unity of style for a whole trilogy

■ the counterpoint between the baby's birth and baptism and the gangsters' deaths

The audience also bring their own mental models to their understanding of the sequence itself. The following schemata may help us to construct our hypothesis of what is going on at different levels of meaning:

■ The signifiers of the Roman Catholic church

■ Our understanding of rites of passage, such as baptism

■ The conventions of gangster films, based on our previous viewings of such films

■ Cross-cutting such as we have seen in other moving image texts as varied as cartoons, soap operas and news programmes

■ Sounds we have recognised in other settings, including everyday ones

■ Novels and short stories we have read or plays and films we have seen

■ Our understanding of what has happened in *The Godfather* so far

In *The Godfather Part II* Coppola uses a similar technique in a grander way: the whole plot consists of two narratives running simultaneously throughout the film. In *The Godfather Part III* the ending also uses a parallel narrative: the sequence in the opera house, where an attempt on Michael's life will take place, is presented in conjunction with the murders of many of the family's enemies at the behest of the new godfather, Vincent Mancini (played by Andy Garcia). Coppola's decision to use these methods creates a unity of style for the whole trilogy.

non-linear structures

We will look at some narrative theorists to understand more about narrative structure from a more holistic perspective.

BINARY OPPOSITION: LÉVI-STRAUSS

The work of the anthropologist Claude Lévi-Strauss (1908–) introduced a tool that emphasised the way a society's works of art, such as films, reveal

conflicts that help us to understand the plot

inherent conflicts. Conflict is caused by opposition. These conflicts are used as part of the unifying structure of the text, as the audience can make sense of these oppositions. How can we explore the structures of the human mind by looking at the evidence produced by social codes and cultural artefacts?

The term binary opposition was coined, following on from the work of Ferdinand de Saussure (1857–1913), the Swiss linguist, to refer to the thematic structures within a text that ultimately condition the narrative. In *The Godfather*, for example, we can see the following oppositions:

The individual	The family
The Church (God)	The Mafia world (Devil)
The Godfather ('good')	The other dons (bad)
War hero	Murderer
The President	The Godfather
Father	Patriarch
Men (active)	Women (passive)
Tom Hagen (calm)	Sonny (impulsive)
Corporate America	The Mafia
The American Dream	The American reality
The Don (benevolent)	Michael (malevolent)
Order (Mafia control)	Chaos (Mafia wars)
Police as protectors	Police as corrupt

These oppositions highlight some of the major themes and characters in the film, but they also point to the conflicts that help us to understand the plot.

These binary oppositions are not simply themes – they are carefully interwoven into the texture of the narrative and condition many aspects of character behaviour.

The Godfather is a perverse myth

NARRATIVE AND MYTH: VOGLER

Christopher Vogler, following on from the work of Joseph Campbell (1904–87), gives an account of Hollywood narratives that sees them as myths, similar to Greek myths and legends and the religious epics and histories of every culture. Films, as an art form, reflect the society in which they are made. Storytelling is basically myth-making and although myths may superficially vary, they all reveal inherent truths about human nature and what society is thinking.

Using Vogler's terms, the argument is as follows. Myths present us with this narrative:

> The hero is introduced in an *ordinary world*, where he *reluctantly* receives a *call to adventure*, and is persuaded by a *mentor* to *cross the first threshold* by encountering *tests, allies and enemies*. He *approaches the inmost cave*, crossing a second threshold, and faces the *supreme ordeal* to receive a *reward*. On *the road back* he crosses a third threshold and experiences a *resurrection* and returns with the *elixir*.

The Godfather retold in this mythic form becomes:

> Michael is a soldier (war hero) in an *ordinary world* – peacetime America. He is *reluctant* to become part of the family business but is persuaded by the love for his father (his *mentor*) to respond to *the call to adventure* by *crossing the threshold* from innocent bystander to protector of his father when he goes to the hospital. Here he is *tested* by *enemies*, in the form of McCluskey, and *approaches the inmost world* of the Mafia when he becomes one of their assassins, the *supreme ordeal*. His *reward* takes him to Sicily where he meets and marries his one true love, Appolonia. After her death he takes the *road back* home to be *resurrected* as the new godfather, receiving the *elixir* of power.

The Godfather is a perverse myth because the family are, to begin with, already evil. The point of this interpretation is that the central narrative is not unfamiliar to us, but the setting is. It transforms the myth to tragedy, and Michael's tragedy has already begun at the commencement of the film as he worships his father, regardless of the world he inhabits. Michael does not receive the usual punishment for evil – death – but becomes the monster himself.

OTHER THEORISTS

It is also worth looking at the work of other theorists who discuss aspects of holistic structure.

Roland Barthes (1915–80) looks at the narrative codes that are at work in structuring a film narrative. These codes are the system of signs, governed by rules and shared by a society. For example, a baptism has particular associations and functions that we all understand and share.

Tzvetan Todorov (1937–) considers narrative as a balance between equilibrium and disruption, the ultimate closure of the narrative and a return to some form of stability. For example, what has happened in the narrative that took the family from the wedding to the baptism and what kind of an equilibrium is at play in the world that the new Don controls?

Vladimir Propp (1895–1970) analysed narratives by looking at character functions in fairy tales and saw many recurring ideas. Our understanding of the tension between character types that we have seen before helps to inform a narrative. For example, what kind of a hero is Michael? What is the function of Luca Brasi?

character

The **narrative** depends on the actions and reactions of characters. In *The Godfather* we have a range of iconic characters, combining **genre archetypes** from pre-1970 and redefining them for the post-70s gangster films.

MICHAEL

Al Pacino was a relatively unknown actor in 1972. He was ideal for casting as Michael as the audience did not have any preconceptions about either him or the character.

a very clearly psychologically defined character

The **hero** of the film is Michael Corleone and the narrative concerns his rise to power. Everything that actually unfolds in the second half of the film relates to decisions either he has made or he is forced to make by people responding to him. He is the causal agent, **protagonist,** and everything else in the narrative leads towards the decisions he must make. The question is, at what cost?

Michael is also a very clearly psychologically defined character. He is an upright and moral man at the beginning of the film: he is a decorated war hero who is courting a WASP (white anglo-saxon protestant) and is rejecting his family's way of life and ethics.

But he is dragged into their moral universe by circumstances that force him to make a decision between remaining in the upright world that he inhabits and protecting the patriarchal figure whom he loves. The moment in the hospital when he kisses his father's hand is Mephistophelian in its implications: he is now on a course from which he will never be able to return.

There are three stages in the development of Michael's character:

1. Michael the war hero
2. Michael in Sicily
3. Michael as the godfather

The character arc takes Michael from hero to villain. It is important for the success of the film that we do not see Michael solely as a villain. We need to understand his motivation, to see what drives him, to make him appear convincingly real.

Robert McKee points out:

> True character is revealed in the choices a human being makes under pressure – the greater the pressure, the deeper the revelation, the truer the choice to the character's essential nature.

Certainly Michael is put under extreme pressure. But the choices he makes are a mixture between good and evil. Consider Michael in outline:

apparent contradictions in his character

Moral	Immoral
Defends his country against Fascism	Is a Mafia mobster – enemy of the state
Upholds the Constitution	Kills a policeman and a gangster
Protects his father against murderers	Breaks his father's heart
Protects his family	Turns his sister into a widow
Is a respectful suitor to Appolonia	Fails to protect Appolonia
Is loyal to his second wife	Lies to his wife

The tension between these two states is what makes the character a complex man. The apparent contradictions in his character are not really all that surprising: we all have character contradictions. In fact, a character who does not have any may not actually be believable. It is important that we be sympathetic to him, we understand him, we can identify with some of his emotions – we may even relate to him.

We are encouraged to rationalise Michael's murderous deeds. The people he kills are mobsters and murderers, and the person he wishes to protect is, after all, his father. But by choosing the same path his father has chosen, namely a violent one and one outside the law, he begins to act in a way that the audience would reject as an option for themselves – except under extreme duress.

DON CORLEONE AND HIS SONS

Casting Brando may have given a contemporary audience conditioned ideas of what to expect from the celebrated actor. His performance stunned most critics – it was not what they had anticipated.

The Don, like Michael, is also a man of contradictions. He appears to be a loving and caring father, yet many aspects of him contradict this view.

The Don's qualities are evident in his sons. Fredo's gentleness, Sonny's

The Don's qualities are evident in his sons

hot temper and ambition, Michael's cool and calculated intelligence. All three of his sons fail.

Fredo, the eldest, is a womanising drunk. The first time we see him, at the wedding, he is already drunk and can barely keep a conversation going with his brother and the new girlfriend. In Las Vegas he is a failure in the casino business: Moe Green points out to Michael that he is so busy with the cocktail waitresses no one can get a drink.

He is weak and inept, and poor of judgement. Before the attempted assassination of his father, Paulie, the regular chauffeur, has not turned up. Fredo says that Paulie is good, yet he is party to the set-up for the assassination. When it happens, Fredo is completely useless and resorts to child mode immediately, sitting on the curb crying.

Fredo is marginalised in all scenes – he acts like a little boy who is not loved. These themes are picked up on in the sequel.

Sonny is quite the opposite. He is strong, masculine, virile, good-humoured. The Don knows about Sonny's adulterous behaviour, yet does nothing to stop him. The Don tells Sonny off for interrupting him during the Sollozzo meeting: he seems more upset that Sonny speaks out of turn, than that he is disloyal to his wife. Numerous times in the film we hear the Don talk of a man's loyalty to his family. When he sees Johnny Fontane in the opening sequence of the film he says that a man who spends no time with his family can never be a real man.

We find out later, from Tom's conversation with Woltz, that Johnny is far from being a family man. He is hardly the godson the Don thinks he is and even Tom knows this. When Johnny arrives at the wedding Tom's cynical remark that he has come because he is in trouble contrasts sharply with the Don's pleasure that he has come all the way from California to attend.

Judgements of people made according to their loyalty to him are indicative of the essentially selfish nature of the Don. He can see them as good people because they pander to his whims; but if we look deeper at what they are really like they are hardly moral characters. The Don's sense of right and wrong is based on fundamental weaknesses in his own character. Either the hypocrisy of these characters is not seen by Don Corleone or it is not important to him.

the essence of the tragedy

The one son who does live by the strict moral code of a family man is Michael. In the scene prior to the Don's death there is a touching moment between father and son when the Don asks if Michael is happy with his wife and children. He later tells Michael that his son looks more like him every day. Later still the Don tells Michael that he wanted more for him but ran out of time.

This scene is important as it contains the essence of the tragedy of both Don Corleone and his son. Michael could have been a different kind of leader, but fate intervened. His father is confessing failure to him just before he dies. At least in Michael the Don recognises his own failure.

The death of Don Corleone is quite an **anti-climax**, considering the nature of the narrative. See Narrative & Form: Opening/Close for an examination of this.

THE FEMALE CHARACTERS

Not surprisingly, the female characters play a marginal role in such a testosterone-charged society. But the very absence of strong female characters is telling in itself. In this patriarchal society they have little power. The genre itself hardly offers much scope for female characters, limited as they largely are to gangster **archetypes** of mothers and molls.

Mama Corleone is the stereotypical mother-figure. She looks after the house, cares for the children, is happy and fun at the wedding, and, what's more, as an obedient wife she never asks about the business. Michael hopes to have a wife like this; he thinks he finds her in Appolonia. She is courteous, virginal and unsophisticated. A passive and childlike figure, but one who was destined to grow into a member of the respectful chorus of mamas who chaperone her during her courting by Michael.

In Kay, however, he has a wife who does ask about the business. Kay is in fact the kind of wife he should have had if he had become Senator Corleone. This mismatch creates an angle of domestic conflict, another obstacle Michael must overcome. Connie, played by Talia Shire, becomes a more dominant character in the rest of the trilogy, especially *Part III*, when she is seen as a vengeful woman, like Medea of Greek tragedy. But in the context of 1972, the women are subsidiary ciphers for the male characters.

point-of-view of ominiscient narration

The Godfather is presented to us in third-person narration. That is, we feel that the camera is objectively detached and is allowing us to sit in on all events. There is in this structure an omniscient narration – i.e., it could go anywhere and see anything. We feel we are able to watch all aspects of the characters' lives. We do not listen to a narrator telling us his or her story in a voice-over from a single point of view.

In closer analysis, however, it is clear that some characters' experiences and points of view have a greater privilege than others'. There is in fact a hierarchy in the narration. For example, at the beginning of the film we are very clearly introduced into the world of Don Corleone – he is the central character and we see life through his eyes to a large degree. He dominates all scenes that he is in: that is the nature of the character and that is the role he fulfils – he is, after all, the king.

Michael, on the other hand, appears very little in the first Act of the film. But when his father is assassinated he becomes increasingly important, and by the third Act we are seeing everything through his gaze. Other characters, such as Fredo or Kay, spend most of their time reacting to the stronger characters. We do not see a scene, for example, showing Fredo having a quiet chat with his father. The narration is restricted in this sense.

Coppola uses a number of other devices in the narration to place Michael at the top of the narrative hierarchy. For example:

■ We see scenes of Michael sitting on his own, thinking

■ We see Michael's reaction outside the hospital when he realises that his own hands are perfectly still but Enzo's are shaking

■ We see Michael in close-up more often as the film progresses

■ The non-verbal communication between Michael and the others and how they respond to him – he is becoming his father

So although *The Godfather* is a film with omniscient narration we can see how the spectator is privileged only within limits set down by the film-maker.

parallelism

We have seen how parallel narrative works by showing contrasting aspects of different scenes and how editing them creates particular meanings. A similar aspect of structure and **style** relates to repetition. A film-maker can bring out particular meanings by repeating certain elements. In a visual form such as a film, the **mise-en-scène** is an ideal vehicle for carrying messages and information throughout the film. For example, there is an abundance of fruit in the mise-en-scène of this film. In particular, oranges are used as part of the unifying design principles:

■ They appear in the dining room of Woltz

■ The Don buys oranges before he is shot

■ When the Don meets the heads of the five families, Don Barzini (who is soon to be recognised as the real danger) plays with an orange picked from the fruit bowl on the table

■ The Don plays with oranges with his grandson – just before he dies

■ The Don appears to be choking on the orange peel in his mouth prior to his heart attack

Dean Tavoularis claims to have used oranges simply as a way of dressing the set – they are a part of the décor. In practice, they become something else, as most of the time they **foreshadow** the violence to come. The spectator is cued to expect something. The oranges become visual **motifs**.

The Don dies in the middle of a small tomato plantation – a setting that seems quite fitting considering the ethnic origin of the character, the centrality of tomatoes in Italian cooking, and the relatively quiet nature of his death.

Sound can also be an important signifier of this kind of parallelism. The soundtrack of Nino Rota's score is used throughout the film to create tension and indicate possible violence. Sombre cello notes create an expectation of violence. Once the film-maker has established the connection between the sound and violence, the spectator will come to expect the same or a similar outcome. Directors can also play with this and violate our expectation, such as the scene in and outside the hospital when we anticipate violence but the full shoot-out does not occur.

Whether the designer or director intends all of these meanings may well be irrelevant. The response of the spectator is what is important here and active spectators make connections, and most of the time they are right to do so, as most of the time good directors are making messages with images.

opening/close

THE OPENING SCENES

The title is shown in plain white on black, with the distinctive solid font and image of the puppeteer holding the strings. We hear the plaintive trumpet of *The Godfather* theme music played very slowly. Fade to black and we hear the first words of the film in a heavy Italian accent: I believe in America.

Coppola puts a major theme into our heads immediately. This film is about America and about what that concept stands for, especially for these immigrant Italians.

Fast fade to a close-up of Bonasera, who tells us his story but adds interesting details.

The first shot is the only shot in the film that employs computerised zoom attached to a BNC Mitchell reflex camera. At the beginning of filming, Coppola and Gordon Willis decided that they would not use the zoom technique, with this exception; they were aiming for a tableau and felt that modern mechanical techniques would interfere with the creation of the correct feeling of a period piece. But this shot was so complicated to achieve that they needed the computerised camera in order to ensure the reverse zoom was slow and consistent.

We first see Bonasera, but as the camera pulls back we see the real subject of the scene from behind and we hear him before we see him clearly. This creates a sense of suspense and tension for the audience: if this is what he sounds like what will he look like? When we do see Brando there is an immediate impact – a match of sound and vision. It is not what we expected: it is not Brando, it is Don Corleone.

The mise-en-scène creates meaning for the audience in a variety of ways. The lighting is low-key – it is difficult to see everything clearly. In fact, when the rushes of this scene were seen by Robert Evans he complained that they were filmed in the dark.

In addition to this, we notice that the visual texture of the opening is very dark indeed, in complete contrast to the other world outside, which we do not see until we are six minutes into the film. The design principle was that the film should be 'brown and black in feeling' according to Willis. This was achieved by careful use of lights, colour and exposure. The technique combined the dark colours of the mise-en-scène of the Don's study – rich and heavy: a large oak desk with leather trim, large dark-brown wooden doors – with that of underexposing the negative. Then when we switch to the wedding we get the feel of old-fashioned footage by using Eastmancolor negative, showing us bright sun and peachy tones in the mise-en-scène. That cut is also combined with a very loud jump to the lively Italian dance music to emphasise the difference between the interior and the exterior environment, both physically and ideologically.

Then Coppola as director thinks on his feet, something he did on numerous occasions on this movie. He found a stray cat on the set and he placed it on Brando's lap to create a much deeper resonance to both the character and the scene. For some it may seem clichéd, as he appears a little like a villain from a Bond movie. Nonetheless, the juxtaposition of the man caressing the cat while he is being asked to murder somebody is still potent.

Then look at Brando's technique in his response to Bonasera: his coy little shake of the head; his scratching of his face as he looks in disgust at Bonasera's request; the stroking of the cat. Brando has to portray a man who has both power and respect. We are invited to like him, even though the supplicant whispering into the ear of the king

we may fear him. The response of everyone else in the room adds to this performance; for example, when the Don stands so does Tom Hagen; Sonny begins to pay attention; Bonasera looks frightened.

Bonasera is forced to whisper his demand: he must not speak loudly of murder, it would hardly be tasteful, given the celebratory circumstances. This also involves him moving to the Don to give us the perfect shot of the supplicant whispering into the ear of the king or pope. Bonasera makes matters worse by asking how much would it cost – the mention of money seems unpalatable to the Don.

The scene presents us with powerful images that are at the heart of the film's narrative, character and themes. The den is like a court to which supplicants come for justice. The signifiers of bowing, kissing the hand of the powerful man, and calling him by an appellation that implies a close guardianship show us the power of the central character in the scene. But the themes of justice, respect and revenge are all part of the overall film. The narrative is about a man who wants justice, respect and revenge – but that man is Michael. The sins of the father are brought upon the child. A true godfather protects his charge by showing him or her the moral, righteous way. The corruption of the role is a central metaphor for the film.

Coppola also uses a startling contrast for effect. The abrupt shift to the wedding and the loud, festive music jolts the audience. The colour scheme of the wedding is distinctive, as we see many soft colours: whites, oranges, peaches. These are in complete contrast to the dark colours of the study. The room is furnished with tasteful wooden blinds. The enclosed chamber, while reeking of wealth on the one hand, is perfect for such furtive and murderous activities. The style of the mise-en-scène allows Coppola to establish a binary opposition within the opening sequence: the innocent and happy (female) exterior, but the serious and grave (male) interior. This is further underlined by the happy, festive, Italian music at the wedding sequence whereas silence reigns in the Don's study.

We see a consummate mix of techniques that are combined by editing to give a vivid portrait of setting, character and theme.

in this confessional there is no forgiveness

THE CLOSING SCENES

In an earlier chapter we examined the parallel narrative used in the famous baptism scene and saw how this prepares us for the contrast of the quiet but equally shocking end. Michael has wiped out all of his enemies in one fell swoop. He now has some unfinished business to attend to with some people who are close to him: Tessio, Carlo and, of course, his wife.

The manner of execution of the first two of these incidents is calm, quiet and emotionless. It is purely business. Again, a façade is drawn over the brutality of what is really happening, just as in the Don's time. Tessio even says as he is led away to be executed that it was only business.

The scene with Carlo is chilling in the portrayal of Michael now as a cold, ruthless, lying murderer. He creates a perfect set-up in which to capture the confession from Carlo. Michael implies amnesty when he emphasises their family link. But to force the confession he gets close to him, gives him a drink, and gives him two plane tickets to Las Vegas. And then he says, in a quiet but firm voice, that telling him he is innocent will insult his intelligence and make him angry.

The use of body language, tone of voice, proximity, all are calculatingly designed to get three words out of Carlo: his confession that it was Barzini.

From that point on, Carlo is dead, for confession is all Michael wants; in this confessional there is no forgiveness, just swift and final punishment. Michael calmly watches as the execution takes place in the car, and walks away like an empty, dead man himself. He has physically changed into the monster he never wanted to be and Pacino's body language signals this hollowness.

The scene with Kay shows an equally frightening man, but this time because of his outburst. When Kay pushes him to answer her question he slams his hand on the desk in anger, and then as his rage dissipates tells her that just this time he'll tell her about his affairs. And then comes the devastating lie, as confident as could be. This is not the Michael we met at the beginning of the film.

The penultimate shot, of Michael being enthroned as the new don accepting supplication from his subjects, is in **medium long shot** through a framed doorway. The study is a shadow of what it was at the beginning of the film: empty, bare, a skeleton, much like Michael, for he is not the benevolent man his father was.

The final shot of Kay, bewildered, shocked, looking in at her husband, as Neri closes the door, suggests the emptiness of Michael's life in the future and her separation from him. Although *The Godfather Part II* continues the saga, *The Godfather* itself as a complete entity resolutely indicates the ultimate despair. The new equilibrium is not a happy or peaceful one.

style

As we saw in our examination of auteur theory (see Background: Director as Auteur), style is something that can be seen as the mark or stamp of the director. In our examination of the opening and closing scenes we saw that style is just as important as narrative and character in creating a complete unity that works on many deep levels.

classical hollywood narration

David Bordwell offers a model to understand narration of films such as *The Godfather*, which he refers to as the classical Hollywood style – sometimes called 'the invisible style'. It is 'invisible' because it is unobtrusive – it is designed to allow spectators to forget that they are watching a piece of technology, to assist with the willing suspension of disbelief.

Major aspects of this style include:

■ The storyline should be clear to the audience – no matter how complicated the plot is

■ There is a clear sense of cause and effect – the film makes sense, it is logical, especially in relation to the realist aesthetic

■ The major causal agent is the main character – or the hero – the narrative happens because he or she acts

■ Psychologically defined characters move towards either achievement of goals or failure

■ The style is relatively objective, although some points of view may dominate

■ There is closure and resolution – there is emotional satisfaction for the audience

THE GODFATHER

a strong sense of cause and effect

■ All major **enigmas** are resolved – we should not walk out of the cinema rewriting the film in our heads

■ Audience pleasures are fulfilled – we are satisfied that we have received value for money, amongst other things

■ **Continuity editing** makes the trick of the cinema invisible

■ There is spatial continuity – usually using the 180° rule

In *The Godfather* we have a strong and dynamic storyline spread sporadically over a five-year period. No matter how often we may move between different locations or jump to different time periods the structure of the film includes specific signifiers to keep us in tune. For example, when Michael moves to Sicily the narrative continues in a clear chronological order. The sense of time passing is created by interweaving the two narratives (America and Sicily) together. The sequence is also framed by two horrific murders (the restaurant in New York and the car bomb in Sicily).

There is a strong sense of cause and effect in the structure of the narrative. In the opening sequence we see a somewhat benign middle-aged man at his daughter's wedding, occasionally doing some business with respectful friends. The Fontane **sub-plot** enables Coppola immediately to establish a number of things about the Don:

■ The way he does business – with intimidation, threats, murder

■ What the phrase, 'I'll make him an offer he can't refuse', actually means in visual terms – we see the blood (buckets of it)

■ The results of his decisions – they hurt people

■ His cold reaction to Tom's solution to the Woltz problem – as a pragmatist he simply sees that he is getting what he wants

Look at the end of the sequence in Woltz's bedroom. The man is screamimg with a mixture of shock and terror. The audience now fully realises what the Don is capable of. Coppola uses a cross-fade, or **dissolve**, to take us back to New York, to a **close-up** of the Don nodding calmly, as if to say, 'Oh well'. The visual **counterpoint** of the blood and the Don tellingly

a strong sense of closure

creates a vivid picture of the real character behind the veneer of respectability.

We hear the Don ask if Tom is tired, and Tom reply that he slept on the plane. He then begins to tell the Don about Sollozzo.

With a very simple technique Coppola achieves a smooth and swift narrative and begins two scenes at the same time. Time has passed very quickly with a simple ellipsis: we do not need to hear Tom tell the Don what happened, we merely see his undisturbed reaction. The next sub-plot has also started. At the end of the very next scene flowers arrive from Johnny, signifying that the Don got what he wanted: Johnny will star in the new picture. Woltz was made an offer he couldn't refuse. Cause and effect; efficiency of style.

The film has a strong sense of closure in narrative terms: all of Michael's enemies are destroyed and he makes the ultimate step towards being the king. The fact that he is even more ruthless than his father is the frightening conclusion.

The major enigmas have now been resolved and we are left with a strong sense of tragedy, which of course was Coppola's starting point: 'This is a story about a king who has three sons.'

For a discussion of the technical aspects of continuity editing see Cinematography.

mise-en-scène

The mise-en-scène is important in the creation of meaning in a film. The term mise-en-scène refers to the aspects of the film that we see in the world of the film, or in the frame on the screen; it literally means 'that which is put into the scene'. The mise-en-scène of a film is not there by accident or whim: it is carefully constructed, like everything else, to contribute to a unifying whole. The mise-en-scène is therefore part of a signifying system.

In the mise-en-scène, therefore, we could examine the following aspects:

THE GODFATHER

a period piece

- ■ Set
- ■ Props
- ■ Costumes
- ■ Performance
- ■ **Dialogue**
- ■ Lighting
- ■ **Special effects**
- ■ **Diegetic sound**
- ■ Camerawork
- ■ **Composition** of the frame

The last two are sometimes analysed separately under the term mise-en-shot.

Many of these aspects are discussed in the earlier analysis of particular scenes or characters. Some further examples are worth considering in this section.

DESIGN, SETTING AND LIGHTING

One of the most difficult aspects of the design of this film was that it was a period piece (from 1945 to 1955) and although the time span between 1945 and 1971 was not immense, it was long enough to cause major problems. America had changed a great deal over the intervening years. Coppola insisted that every aspect of design had to be authentic so that the realism was convincing, so literally thousands of pieces of set and costume design were made, bought or borrowed.

Verisimilitude is not the only design principle, however. The dress code of the Don, for example, had to reflect his character: he is a man of immense power and wealth, but he wears what he needs to, depending upon the situation, because to him the clothes do not make the man. So we do not always see the Don in suits or tuxedos but sometimes dressed in the shabbiest of clothes as he seems to potter about the house or den, and increasingly so as he gets older and relinquishes power. Michael conversely

mise-en-scène

switches from 'preppie'-style clothes to much more formal attire as he becomes the new godfather.

In locations, Coppola needed New York. The real locations for most external scenes give the film a depth it would otherwise not have. In the scene where Paulie is murdered, for example, we observe the scene in extreme long shot. This distancing is itself effective, but what gives the shot its extra power visually is the head of the Statue of Liberty peeking over the fields, almost watching the awful event. Real locations are used throughout the film, for example:

■ The assassination attempt on the Don was filmed in a street in New York's Little Italy

■ To create the right festive atmosphere for the Christmas scenes, shots were taken outside Radio City Music Hall and Best and Co.

■ The exterior of Woltz's mansion was the Guggenheim estate

Colour was an important design principle of the film. There are frequent contrasts between white and pastel shades, associated with the female world, and much darker sets that are predominantly the world of the men. For example, the interior décor of Connie and Carlo's apartment is a mixture of whites, fawns and peaches; it tells the audience that this is her domain, and so it is not surprising that he is hardly ever there. This world is smashed up at the point when Carlo rejects this in order to set up Sonny's assassination.

Most of the sets that the men talk in are dark in colour and dimly lit. For example:

■ the Don's study
■ Woltz's studio
■ Genco's office
■ Sollozzo meeting with Hagen
■ the meeting of the dons
■ the meeting between Michael and Carlo at the end

the meetings of men are dark and furtive

The meetings of men are dark and furtive in this world of murderers and deceivers. Even the outdoor **sequences** are mostly during overcast days, or when it is snowing, or at night. By contrast, the Sicily sequence is bright and sunny. It represents a new world for Michael, one where he can get away from the Mafia world of his father.

The lengths Coppola and his team went to in creating these worlds reflect the change in the realist aesthetic by 1971. Audiences were now much more sophisticated in their understanding of film and higher expectations were placed on film-makers to get minute details right.

For analysis of particular scenes in detail see Narrative & Form: Opening/Close.

cinematography

THE SHOT

Camera distance

The use of distance is an elementary form of film grammar. The director has at his or her disposal a variety of different **shots**, depending upon how far away the camera is from the central action, to convey an appropriate meaning.

Coppola uses the **medium shot** and the **medium close-up** for many of the scenes involving people talking, as these invite intimacy between **text** and audience; we are being privileged by listening in on these conversations. If we look at the scene when Michael is talking to his father, we see a very simple style being used. Coppola uses the shot/reverse shot technique: this involves cutting between the two men talking by using **over-the-shoulder shots** and medium shots. When Michael asks his father what is bothering him, instead of moving the camera, Brando moves and sits next to Pacino. We now have a medium close-up and a **two-shot** – a much more intimate shot for a heartfelt confession from the Don. It is a perfect match between content and style.

At the funeral we can see **cuts** between **medium long shots** (of the congregation) and **close-ups** (of Michael). The effect of this is to make the audience ask: 'What is Michael thinking? What is Michael plotting?' Like

the car peppered with holes

Michael, we are expecting an attempt on his life, as the Don has foreseen. We are now drawn into the mind of the **protagonist** much more as we are asking the same questions he is asking and seeing the congregation through his eyes, from his **point of view**.

The scene of Sonny's assassination uses a variety of shots. It begins in **extreme long shot** as we see the cars approach the toll-booth. But we are quickly taken inside Sonny's car with close-ups so that the audience can realise what is happening at the same time as the character, again employing point of view and reaction shots. When the shooting occurs, Coppola switches from inside the car to medium shots outside the car, **cross-cut** with close-ups of the guns, so that we can feel the full force of the assault. To finish, we have a **montage** of the devastation: the toll-booth wrecked, the car peppered with holes, Sonny's bloody body. The last shot is a **long shot** of the whole carnage, a sort of full stop to the scene. The shock effect of this scene owes much to the combination of shots and the way that the director has lulled us into the middle of it and then allowed us to stand back in horror.

Camera angle

A director can choose from variations of straight on, **high angle** or **low angle**. For example, a low angled shot of Michael at the funeral of his father reinforces the position of power he now holds. Conversely, a high angled shot does the same thing at the end of the scene in Las Vegas. When deciding if a low angle shot indicates strength and a high angled shot indicates weakness the director must consider the whole effect of the shot – what else is contributing to the effect, for example, lighting, distance, movement?

Look at the scene in the Don's den when Sonny is considering what to do next after the McCluskey incident. In medium shot we see various people standing around, with Michael sitting in the large leather armchair; the camera is at eye level with those talking, so looking down on Michael, who is in a weak position. But when Tom Hagen sits down, behind Michael, the camera goes down with him to now be at eye level with Michael. Why? Because Michael is about to hatch the plot that leads to his downfall, and as he explains his plans the camera can move in a slow **dolly** towards Michael and have a medium close-up at his eye level and thereby make him appear stronger. Coppola's skill is that he makes the shot unobtrusive, but forceful nonetheless.

Camera movement

Coppola uses a **zoom** only once in the whole film, and even then it is very slow (and computer operated) – this is the first shot of the film. Coppola shies away from excessive camera movement towards a more studied vision. Remember, much of this film is actually taken up with people talking, listening or watching and excessive camera movement would be intrusive or might even attract attention to itself.

The director also avoids **hand-held shots** and **crane shots**. The reason for this is that he does not want to be obtrusive, especially as many of the scenes are interiors. But he will use slow **tracks**, dollies, slow **pans** or tilts to carefully guide the spectator's eyes. For example, when people are moving in or around the Long Island Mall, where the Don lives, the camera usually follows them slowly and discreetly.

CONTINUITY EDITING

Hollywood has developed the technique of the invisible style over decades, from the early days of D.W. Griffiths right up to the present. The major aim of this style is to engage the audience as completely as possible in the world of the film so that we **willingly suspend disbelief**. **Continuity editing** attempts to use time and space coherently in order to present a linear **narrative** with clarity and meaning. It also assists in the achievement of **realism** as it makes the audience forget the camera as it tries to be unobtrusive, except in moments that require particular techniques.

See The Shot: Camera Distance for two techniques used in continuity editing:

■ shot/reverse shot
■ point of view shot

cinematography

Types of edit

Coppola uses a variety of edits including **fade-ins**, **fade-outs** and **dissolves** in order to keep the narrative flowing and maintain the audience interest. He even uses elaborate montage sequences to create a segue from one period of time to another or from location to location, for example, when Michael leaves for Sicily. Most edits are carefully chosen to assist with continuity editing.

Match on action

This technique, also known as a match-cut, involves the matching of action at the end of one shot with the continued flow of action in the next shot, thereby giving the impression of continuity, just as we would expect in real life. This occurs throughout a well-made film and is not difficult to spot, but other aspects of matching action are a little more complicated. A director can also match action between cuts to make connections between similar forms, characters or events. For example, there is a match dissolve at the end of the infamous horse's-head scene. We see Woltz scream in horror in reaction to what he has just realised, and a series of cuts takes us to an extreme long shot of the Woltz mansion as his screams fill the night air. The dissolve then takes us to a close-up of the Don as Tom Hagen has just told him of the event. The connection between the evil act and the real perpetrator is then made, and when the Don swiftly and unemotionally moves on and asks if Tom is not too tired, we are given a deep insight into his character in a split second.

Spatial continuity: the 180° degree rule

This is one of the major rules of continuity editing. The director needs to establish clear spatial relationships in the **frame** so that the audience do not become confused. So a camera on a set will be carefully placed each time in order not to cross an imaginary line drawn in the action, otherwise the audience would be miscued by characters apparently looking in the wrong direction. If the camera stays one side of the line (in its 180° sphere of action) spatial logic remains.

The camera stays on one side of the action within a particular scene. For example, in the den in the first scene we never see a view from the corner

this shot is about powerlessness

on the right-hand side. Coppola sticks to camera positions that either face the desk and the window or move to the left-hand side.

COMPOSITION

In addition to the techniques outlined above, the director also has to consider the **composition** of the frame: where are constituent elements of the shot placed in relation to each other? For example, part of the power of the final shot of the film is that Kay is placed centre-centre in the frame and is then framed again within the doorway. This shot is about powerlessness and being closed down – this shot shows despair.

A close look at scenes that contain the Don would show that he is frequently placed in a powerful position when he is playing at being the Don. Conversely, scenes in which he is not in power-mode show him to be considerably weaker. Compare the opening scene, where he is sitting behind a large desk and on his throne, to a later scene in the study when Michael has taken over the reins, where the Don is marginalised to the side, wandering about like a lost old man, feeding his fish. Again the placing of characters in particular parts of the screen and in relation to particular objects has an effect on how the audience read, or interpret, that character.

SOUND

As film is such a strongly visual medium, we often forget the importance of aural signifiers. Just as directors very carefully frame their shots and consider what is put into the picture, so they make careful decisions concerning the soundtrack. There are two basic ways of considering sound in a film:

1. **Diegetic sound** Is it in the world of the film, such as a train passing by or a clock ticking, which the characters in this world would hear? These sounds assist the realism of the film.

2. **Non-diegetic sound** Is it outside the world of the film, such as the music soundtrack, which the characters would not hear? The soundtrack generally creates a mood or feeling within the audience – it can quieten them down and soothe them, or liven them up and create tension or excitement.

cinematography

One of the most intense **sequences** in the film is the shooting of Sollozzo and McCluskey in the restaurant. Michael goes to the toilet to pick up the gun, but as he leaves he holds his hands to his head as if to show the weight of the moment that is about to occur. But we also hear a passing train which, of course, we assume to be in the diegesis of the film; in other words, we assume it is a train passing by the restaurant and Michael can hear it. When he takes his seat again, Michael is placed in tight close-up as Sollozzo speaks to him in Italian. We are aware of the momentous nature of this point in the narrative: Michael is about to cross the line into his father's world. As the decisive moment approaches, another train passes by, this time the sound grows and grows and almost completely drowns out Sollozzo's monologue. But the sound of the train acts in a different way now; it is not simply a diegetic sound, it reinforces what is going through Michael's mind and has a direct effect upon the audience. It builds up the tension until it finally explodes into gunshots and murder.

Sound is also very useful in continuity editing, most obviously in the use of soundtrack music to take us from one scene to the next. But look at the way Coppola moves us out of the scene in which Don Corleone dies. We finish in long shot seeing the prostrate figure of the dead Don; we realise in the silence what has happened in a perfectly judged **anti-climax**. We also hear the toll of a bell and as we dissolve into the next scene we realise that we are hearing the diegetic bells of the Don's funeral. This is a good example of how sound can be expertly used to assist in the creation of the invisible style.

SPECIAL EFFECTS

In a film with so much gunfire it is hardly surprising that **special effects** (or SFX) are an important area of creating the illusion of the reality of the violence. One of the problems for this film when it went on general release was that the violence was so graphic. Coppola was quite clear in his mind what the priority was: realism.

Again, look at many of the scenes of violence to see how the special effects create the illusion of murder, for example, the horse's head in Woltz's bed; the bullet-riddled body of Sonny; the shots through the heads of McCluskey and Sollozzo; the shot in the eye of Moe Green; the devastating destruction in the baptism sequence. It was partly the skill of the special effects team that helped to create such a buzz around the film's first release; audiences were stunned by the authenticity of the violence that they saw.

DIALOGUE

The Godfather is a film that needs to convince us of a certain reality: that of the Mafia. The **dialogue** is an important part of this realism. There are a number of ways in which this is achieved.

The characters frequently speak in Italian, with subtitles for non-Italian speakers. Coppola chooses this method for verisimilitude – it would be against the realism of the film if we didn't hear Italian at all and depended solely on heavy Italian accents. In films of previous decades it would not be uncommon for all nationalities to speak in English even if they were speaking to fellow compatriots without an English-speaking person present. It also makes the point that the younger members of the Corleone family are second-generation Italians. On two occasions Michael deliberately opts to speak English: in the restaurant with Sollozzo; and in Sicily when he first meets Appolonia's father. He is more comfortable in his own tongue.

Some aspects of their Italian vocabulary, however, come not just from their ethnic origins. It is the language of a hierarchical organisation, such as an army. So we hear terms such as *consiglieri* (counsellor) or *caporegimes* (sub-divisions within the family) and, of course, godfather (the chief of command). This language gives a particular flavour to the nature of the Mafia: they are well organised with clear-cut roles and ranks.

Slang and swearing are also frequently used, especially as humour between men. The language of particular men can be coarse and vulgar and it is often a common aspect of male bonding and male society; the Mafia is no different. Sonny is fond of this kind of talk, Michael never uses it, so the style of language differentiates these brothers.

The language of the Latin mass is also predominant in one scene in particular. The solemnity of this language contrasts strongly with the ugly images on the screen.

Finally, there is the delivery by the actors and the way they change dialogue by the nature of its expression. See The Performative, below.

THE PERFORMATIVE

The style of acting in the film is derived from the work of the Russian actor, teacher and theatre director, Konstantin Stanislavsky, and his adherents in America, notably Stella Adler and Lee Strasberg. See Background: Key Players' Biographies on Brando and Pacino.

With at least two adherents of the **Method** in the cast, Brando and Pacino, and a sympathetic director, it is hardly surprising that the style of acting is significant in this film. This type of acting relies heavily on a natural and convincing portrayal of character, inside and out: a combination of psychological truth and technical expertise. The aim is to have a much more convincing, three-dimensional performance, one that is more realistic. The dominant mode of **representation** in films is realism, and this is particularly true of The Godfather.

The hallmarks of this style of acting involve:

■ Immersing oneself as an actor into the thoughts, feelings and personality of the role – to become the character

■ Using actors' business as naturally as the character would – hence the Method actor always seems to be doing something else – or nothing

■ Using personal experience to inform the performance – to be introspective and internalised

■ Low-key performances – the actor can often seem very still

■ The use of phatic aspects of communication – the actor will stutter, pause, hesitate, repeat, grope for the sentence

■ The actors speaking over each others' lines – just as we do in real life

■ Hand and facial gestures that are small and specific – even idiosyncratic to the character

■ Being able to move the audience who are completely convinced of the character and therefore the situation

Brando would stay in character for long periods

■ The actor immersing himself or herself in the part so much that he or she remains in role even when they are not shooting

■ The actor spending time with real people like the one being portrayed, and in the real world in which they live – sometimes even being with them for weeks

■ Make-up, prosthetics, padding, etc., to look as real as the character would be

■ Putting on, or losing, weight to look the right shape or size

■ The actor's ability to improvise to get to the truth of the character or bring the right feel to the dialogue

Examples of this type of acting are evident in almost every scene in which Brando and Pacino appear.

We have already mentioned Brando's mannerisms in the first sequence (see Narrative & Form: Opening/Close). At the scene with all the dons meeting we are never quite sure when Don Corleone will speak – his hand gestures and glances keep throwing the audience. But when he does want to make the most important point he is forceful and direct in his gaze. When he seems to be relaxing he is always doing something: patting the cat; peeling an orange; drinking wine; feeding the fish in the aquarium. His gestures when he is ill are absolutely minimal, in some cases almost undetectable. He frequently pauses and breaks up his lines – look at the screenplay available on the Internet, which captures verbatim what he says or grunts.

On the set Brando would stay in character for long periods, wandering around, mumbling to himself like an old man. He wore 'dental plumpers', flesh-coloured acrylics that fit between the mouth and teeth of the actor, to pad out his features and make him look older and more distinctive. He wore earplugs so that he could concentrate on his lines. He met real members of the Mafia to find out how they spoke to each other; he even modelled Vito Corleone's voice on a recording of one of them with a rough, husky voice. He lost weight to play the part of Vito as a forty-six-year-old in the first scene – so much so that he had to put twenty pounds back on prior to the first day of shooting.

there are now numerous versions

the director's cut

Many stories have circulated about the making of this film; one of the more interesting for us is the dispute between Evans and Coppola concerning the final edit. Exactly who was responsible for the cut that made it to the premiere in March 1972? Even now this is hotly disputed.

For all directors the final cut is of paramount importance. In this day and age it is a crucial part of the marketing tool of a Hollywood studio to have the first exhibition cut and then follow it up a few years later with the director's cut. Hollywood's view is: why sell a film once when you can sell it ten times?

The idea of a director's cut for *The Godfather* is further complicated by the fact that there are now numerous versions, including part of the trilogy. There are the following in existence:

■ The original cut that premiered in New York and was first on release

■ *The Godfather: the Complete Epic*: this is the combination of Parts I and II in mostly chronological order that was broadcast by NBC as a four-part mini-series in November 1977. This is also known as *Mario Puzo's The Godfather: The Complete Novel for Television* and *The Godfather Saga* and it contains some extra footage containing violence and nudity

■ *The Godfather Trilogy*: a re-edited version of all three films into mostly chronological order

The new edits involving *The Godfather Part I* include:

■ A framing device that had Michael thinking back to all that happened in flashback

■ Extra footage of Connie's wedding **sequence**

■ Extra scenes in Hollywood

■ The Don listening to Tom about his visit to Woltz and instructing him to send Luca Brasi

the director's cut

- An extra scene with Michael and Kay in their hotel room in New York when Michael phones home and pretends he is in New Hampshire
- A restored sequence involving the death of Genco, the original *consiglieri*, which reinforces the idea that Tom was not yet in the post
- A scene in the hospital corridor when the family go to visit Genco on his deathbed and the Don intimates that he has plans for Michael, but his son is cold in his response as he believes that his father is referring to the family business
- An extra scene in Sicily with Michael, Calo and Fabrizio resting under a tree – Michael refers to his father as a *pezzonovante*
- Many of Sonny's scenes during the section of the film where he was in charge were cut – James Caan was not happy about the final cut as he claimed many of his more subtle moments as an actor were lost – and some ideas about masculinity were explored
- Scenes suggesting that Clemenza was a traitor
- Extra footage in the scene where the *caporegimes* are told that Michael is in charge and Tom notices the sudden importance of Neri and Rocco
- An extra scene with Michael talking to his father in the garden where Michael says that although his father gave his word that he would not break the peace, Michael did not
- A final scene showing Kay in church lighting a candle for Michael's soul

There are a number of errors in continuity of narrative in the final film. When Coppola first saw the film with an audience he said it was unbearable as he could only see the mistakes. To a first-time audience, however, these subtleties are almost certainly lost.

Two of the important cuts are the flashback and the sequence with Kay in the church at the end. As it stands it is now much more chilling as we are left with her being deceived and marginalised with ease by Michael yet we do not see her reaction. We are left wondering what kind of life she has ahead of her with this monster.

a slur on their Italian heritage

Perhaps the most interesting cut of all is to do with the nomenclature of the gangster family. The names Mafia and Cosa Nostra are never used in *The Godfather Part I*. This was because the Italian-American Civil Rights League made such a fuss over the intention to film the novel, which they believed was a slur on their Italian heritage, that Al Ruddy, the producer, acquiesced on this point in order to get the project moving without too much adverse publicity.

contexts

ideology

Consider the following questions or statements:

■ Which is more important to you: your country or your family?

■ Do you believe in unconditional love?

■ The father should be the head of the family.

■ Murder is justifiable if the people you are killing are murderers themselves.

■ Our ethnic background is the most important aspect of our identity.

■ Do the ends ever justify the means?

Our views on issues such as these will partly determine how we interpret *The Godfather*. They are issues that get to the heart of our own personal ideology.

Consider the following questions:

■ Is Michael right to enact revenge on Sollozzo and McCluskey?

■ Has Michael served a purpose to society by wiping out the other dons?

■ Is it better for Kay to know nothing about her husband's business?

■ Is the Don a good father?

■ Is the Italian community slurred by this film?

Ideology refers to the system of ideas, values and beliefs that an individual, group or society holds to be true, valid or important. To analyse ideology we need to look at, amongst other things, representations, character behaviour and actions, contemporary issues and the moral universe of the film.

a world whose existence many people denied

NATIONALITY

One of the major representations is that of nationality. What does it mean to these characters to be Sicilian, Italian or American? Historically the north of Italy exploited the south and this is certainly one of the main reasons why so many southern Italians emigrated to the USA. Both Puzo and Coppola had their origins in northern Italy but they did extensive research in order to get the feel of this particular Italian community right.

First of all, one of the reasons Coppola was given this film was that he was of Italian descent and this culture was important to him. It was an attempt by Robert Evans, the Paramount executive in charge of production, to assuage the Italian community whom he rightly anticipated might object to the possible racial stereotyping in the film. The Italian-American Civil Rights League, amongst others, feared that Italian-Americans would be portrayed as a bunch of murdering gangsters who lived outside the law of the land and brought with them a cultural and moral world that was anti-democratic. The IACRL contention was simply that they were the opposite: honest and law-abiding Americans who were contributing much to their New World. Many denied the existence of the Mafia.

The fact that they were vociferous in their objections to the film, rather than to the novel that had been published two years earlier, points to the belief amongst many that moving-image texts are potentially more damaging than literary ones: if you can see it, then the representation might just be more convincing. Remember Coppola was creating a world whose existence many people denied, certainly in that form. The Mafia themselves had denied everything for decades. *The Godfather* created this world more convincingly than any previous film and set the standards for others to follow, such as *Goodfellas* (Scorsese, 1990), *A Bronx Tale* (De Niro, 1993) and *Casino* (Scorsese, 1995).

To what extent does an audience accept the fictional text as a reality, or at least as a version of the truth? Such concerns get to the heart of the relationship between cinema and society. Coppola's answer is seen in the dramatic change in the narrative between novel and screenplay. The film makes the concept of the family much more central to the driving force of the story, and at the same time allows for a sympathetic portrayal of these characters in terms that we can compare to a Shakespearean or Greek tragedy. In turn, this treatment opens up another debate, which asks: how can we be sympathetic to these men who are simply thugs and murderers beyond the law?

The insistence on the realism of the Italian community could be seen to be at the expense of portraying any other racial representations. There is nothing in the film, for example, that attempts to reflect any Black American issues of the day (with the exception of one derogatory reference). The realism of *The Godfather* is so convincing that we can never forget that the main characters are Italian as it is so important to them. The insistence by Coppola, against studio wishes, to film in New York and Sicily is a testament to this. The production goes to great pains to put the Italian aspect at the forefront: the mise-en-scène; the theme music; the dialogue; the accents.

GANGSTERS

In some ways the film can be seen within its genre, as many gangster films are dependent upon portraying 'hoods' who are Italian because the real-life figures on whom they are based were indeed Italian: *Little Caesar* (Mervyn LeRoy, 1930); *Scarface: Shame of a Nation* (Howard Hawks, 1932); *St Valentine's Day Massacre* (Roger Corman, 1967); *The Brotherhood* (Martin Ritt, 1968); *The Untouchables* (Brian De Palma, 1987). But how authentic are any of these portrayals, and do we see the main characters first as gangsters, and their Italian background as irrelevant? It is also an important aspect of the genre that the main character be attractive to the audience, despite the fact that he is a murderer.

Real-life gangsters were apparently thrilled with *The Godfather* and considered the representation a flattering one. This alone causes disquiet amongst certain commentators.

By its nature the gangster genre is quite conservative. Although these men live outside the law and make their living, or fortune, from immoral and illegal acts, their success is short-lived. They are always either brought to justice or killed and the moral message of the film is clear: crime does not pay (at least, not until the films of the 1990s). This is partly historical, as

Coppola has made these men sympathetic

the Motion Picture Production Code, aka the **Hays Code**, was set up in 1930 as a form of censorship in reaction to public moral panic following sex scandals. In the subsequent years the brief of the Hays Office expanded until it became a powerful voice in many areas of ideological concern; it was not abolished until 1968, just three years before *The Godfather* went into production.

Coppola has made these men sympathetic to us. His skill lies in a combination of the realist aesthetic and the connotations of the structure of a tragic **narrative** that complicates the ideological **closure** of the text. The film has a triumphant **hero** at the end: he has vanquished his enemies and placed himself swiftly and deftly into pre-eminent position as the gangland leader of the USA. The audience is conscious of what motivates Michael in the first place – to protect his father and, now, to protect his family. Michael's seeming lack of interest in money for its own sake makes him much more appealing. Michael also cares for his family and spends time with them, unlike Sonny. Michael has a strict sexual ethical code like his father but unlike Fredo. So each time we compare Michael with his family he always seems better.

But Coppola can't simply leave it at that, as he is also morally aware of the ideological consequences of this resolution. He still follows the **conventions** of the genre by establishing beyond doubt in the audience's mind that this power and authority come at a price, one that most people would reject. Michael is a murderer and a liar. His deception, however, extends to his family. It is the beginning of the end, which is potently followed through in the rest of the trilogy. A central value that his father adhered to has been abolished.

MASCULINITY

The film is not just about Italians – it is about Italian men. The society these men lived in was highly patriarchal: the men decided what happened in the lives of their families and the women were marginalised. Indeed, the portrayal of women is of childminders, cooks and sexual objects. The two leading female roles show one to be a hysterical, spoilt brat (Connie), and the other to be a simplistic and misguided fool (Kay).

ideology

If we look at the last scene of the film we can see many of these elements. The ease with which Michael can lie to both Connie and Kay over the murder of his brother-in-law is significant in itself, but it is Kay's response that is also very telling: she breathes a sigh of relief and suggests they have a drink.

The patriarch has given his word and the obedient wife believes him. In the world in which Michael reigns there can be no room for weakness. He is merely following the example his father set by not allowing business to be discussed at the dinner table, except his wife is not Italian and does not share the world view of Mama Corleone, who would never think of asking such questions. Within her cultural heritage of the proletariat of Southern Italy, there were clearer distinctions between the roles of the husband, the breadwinner, and the wife, the housemaker.

The way in which Sonny casually abuses his position to be adulterous is simply smirked at by Tom Hagen and referred to as 'comedy' by the Don. His wife again is marginalised to the position of childminder and cook and is quite helpless to do anything about this. Sonny does not share his father's moral values in this area, but Michael does.

The role of Appolonia in the mid-Act **sub-plot** is also of interest. Michael travels to his father's homeland in Sicily to gain protection and takes himself a wife, but the New World interferes and she ends up being brutally murdered for her liaison with the Don's son.

The Don's adherence to the idea that a real man must spend time with his wife and children is repeated on a number of occasions. The misogynistic world of these men is rationalised by their belief that they are providing for their family and it is safer for their loved ones not to know anything. Yet the contradictions within this are not acknowledged.

Luca Brasi, when thanking the Don for being invited to the wedding, says that he hopes their first child will be male. He obviously believes that this will impress the Don.

The Don also inculcates masculine pride in his sons. When he is advising Michael in the garden **sequence** he comments that women and children can be careless, but men cannot.

| a metaphor for America

It can be argued of course that the Don is not a good father because of this ideological indoctrination. He has created a family that ignores the original codes of the Mafiosi: remain loyal to your wife, make your family the central core of your being.

In his meeting with Johnny Fontane the Don can't see through Johnny's lies when he asks him if he spends time with his family, but he can see that he is weak when he cries.

AMERICA

In our study of ideology we can also look at some important contemporary issues for Coppola and his audience. The two major political issues of the day were the Vietnam War and the Watergate scandal and they both inform the film ideologically. The narrative itself is set in 1945–51, a period of prosperity and affluence for the USA. But Coppola uses this narrative as a metaphor for America itself, and not that of 1945, but that of the early 1970s. It was a period when America was seriously questioning its leaders in many ways.

The Vietnam War was very unpopular and was a war that Hollywood addressed over the years, capturing the mood of the public, including Coppola's own *Apocalypse Now* (1979). The people's discontent with their leaders was not lost on the director and he maintained that the film, and the trilogy, was a metaphor for America.

Consider the conversation between Kay and Michael after he seeks her out a year after his return to the USA: Michael suggests she is naïve in thinking that senators or presidents don't have people killed.

This short exchange would have been read as a subtext by an audience of the time. There was outcry that the president was sending countless young men to their deaths to avoid an embarrassing climbdown from a war they should never have entered in the first place. There may also be a resonance here of Michael's rejection of his past commitment to active service during the Second World War. (In *The Godfather Part II* we learn that the Don was against him joining up as it was not their fight.)

an Old World form of justice

The 1972 Watergate scandal concerned the illegal activities of President Nixon to infiltrate the Democratic headquarters in Washington; even when found out, the president did everything he could to cover up the crime. The public again lost their trust in their politicians, especially in the patriarchal figure of the president. These exalted figures were no better than burglars and common criminals, yet they were supposed to defend the virtues of American law and the Constitution.

The opening of the film clearly sets up these issues. The new American has adhered to the rules of his adopted country as he believed in democracy and justice and the American way. But it failed him just as the president failed the audience of 1972. Don Corleone is quick to pick up on the central issue.

The Don of course represents an Old World form of justice, one that existed in Sicily when the peasants needed protection from governments and policemen who were unjust. The original conception of the Mafia was that of local justice: it was swift and it was easily understood. The existence of the Don in the New World occurs because things are no different in America if you have been marginalised in the first place – an idea that was to be examined more thoroughly in *The Godfather Part II*.

The Don is in opposition to the *pezzonovante* – the petit bourgeois of the ruling classes, the *nouveau riche* – and he has instilled this in his son. Michael sees politicians in this light: he acknowledges that he is just another *pezzonovante* where his father wished him to be a senator or governor.

It would be a view resonant with the audience. America's distrust of politicians has remained ever since.

Another aspect of the social period of the time is that of the family itself. It was a time when many Americans felt that the nuclear family was disintegrating and that some conventional values were being lost. To this audience the Don and Michael would appear to be morally upright and bastions of an order that should be maintained.

Conversely the film could be read as a rejection of the family and an

the dream can be seen to be bankrupt

indictment of a society that remains true to such archaic and old-fashioned values, especially after post-1960s America.

THE AMERICAN DREAM

Perhaps the greatest attack of the film is that upon the American Dream. This concept is based on the ideological belief in the merits of capitalist America: that a man may be born in the gutter but can make it to be president with hard work and adherence to the American ethics enshrined in the Constitution; that America has a yellow-brick road and you just have to find it by conforming to the ideology of the land of the free. This dream, of course, has been perpetuated and popularised by Hollywood for the entirety of its existence. As far back as 1917, President Woodrow Wilson declared that the country needed Hollywood to sell America: to sell its products; to sell its culture; to sell its ideology; to sell its dream.

If the film is seen as a metaphor for corporate America, as Coppola has suggested, then the dream can be seen to be bankrupt. If we cannot depend upon the forces of law and order, if the politicians are not moral and upright, if the only way to get justice is to go to a Mafia hood, then society is clearly dysfunctional. Corporate America is interested not in the people but in itself. Its ideology is based upon greed and self-interest, yet hidden behind a mask of morality and ethics that defends the family as the centre of the civilised world.

The Old Testament morality of an eye for an eye is central to this world view. Don Corleone sees himself as the defender of honest men in the scene with Bonasera. He defends the little man against the ineptitude of the judicial system, and even sees himself as the judge and jury with a keen sense of justice: he does not see himself as a murderer.

Michael takes these matters even further when he asks where it says that you can't kill a cop, justifying the murder as moral because the cop is crooked, almost as if the Mafia are providing a service.

genre

The gangster genre has always been popular in Hollywood history – until the 1960s when it went into a serious decline. From D.W. Griffith's *The Musketeers of Pig Alley* (1912), the genre continued through the 1930s with star vehicle classics for James Cagney (such as *The Public Enemy*, 1931, and *The Roaring Twenties*, 1939) and Edward G. Robinson (*Little Caesar*, 1930), then into the 1940s with the introduction of *film noir* style and then into the 1950s with social realist texts such as *On the Waterfront* (1954).

What is a gangster film? The term itself suggests that these films are about gangs, but most of the films are really about individuals who happen to be in a gang. It is the nature of the hero that is fascinating about these films because the gangster is defined by what he does, namely rob and kill. From this starting point we can see that the genre is really a combination of action (story) and character, and the motivation of these characters ultimately leads us to the themes, in other words, what the film is really about.

The genre has strict conventions but it is what happens within the formula that makes each film interesting. Another Robert McKee maxim applies: give the audience what they want but not in the way they expect it. Although the audience have a fairly good idea of the kind of story they are going to get, there is quite a range of variations on the theme. Consider the following films: *Angels with Dirty Faces* (1938), *On the Waterfront* (1954), *Bonnie and Clyde* (1967), *The Godfather* (1972), *Reservoir Dogs* (1991) and *Heat* (1995). Although they all belong to the same genre, they demonstrate a number of major differences. There is a wide variety of representations of the gangster; the rise-and-fall has a different trajectory; the social issues have different emphases. As with all genres, the gangster genre is a dynamic paradigm that has adapted to changing times.

Even within contemporary periods the variety is wide: in the 1990s we had films such as *Goodfellas* (1990), *The Godfather Part III* (1990), *New Jack City* (1991), *Bugsy* (1991), *Reservoir Dogs* (1991), *A Bronx Tale* (1993), *Carlito's Way* (1993), *The Usual Suspects* (1995) and *Casino* (1995).

There are also major differences between films from different cultures, such as the Japanese *yakuza* films. Ridley Scott exploited those differences when he explored the cultural clash between Japan and America in *Black Rain* (1989).

The other variable is the precise nature of the gangster himself. Even looking at the work of a single star shows a wide variety of characters. For example, compare James Cagney's portrayal of Rocky Sullivan in *Angels with Dirty Faces* and that of Cody Jarrett in *White Heat* (1949). The former is a very sensitive portrait of the gangster that charts the life of an essentially decent man who crosses the line to the other side because of adverse circumstances; but our sympathy is with him right up to the heartbreaking finale as he walks to the gas chamber. The latter, however, is an Oedipal psychopath who kills with ease, and his death atop the gas tower is a relief – 'On top of the world, Ma.'

In *The Godfather* we can see that ideas from both of these films are explored: the nature and nurture debate that is examined in Sullivan's character; and the establishment of a new order by the ruthless destruction of the old one, as exemplified by Jarrett. Michael begins *The Godfather* as a decorated war hero who rejects his family background. But when he does change because of his adherence to these particular family values, he is even more ruthless than his father and completely annihilates the old order. Is Michael like this because of his experience, or does the extremity of his revenge indicate something much more deep-rooted about his character? Is Michael after revenge only, or is he politically changing the way things will be done from now on?

APPEAL OF THE GENRE

Why was this genre so popular? For a start, the gangster film began life by being rooted in reality and in the well-documented lives of gangsters. The conventional use of newspaper headlines to punctuate the story is a testament to this. In some cases journalists were employed to write the script, such as Ben Hecht on *Scarface: Shame of a Nation* (1932) and *Kiss of Death* (1947). The detached voice-over narration also gave these films a sense of documentary or newsreel footage, for example, the

Dillinger films (1945, 1973) and the influential *The Untouchables* television series of the 1960s.

The Godfather also uses the convention of newspaper headlines as a narrative ellipsis just after the mid-Act climax showing its roots in the genre.

But the popularity of the genre lies mainly in the following:

1. The exciting nature of the narrative
2. The charismatic characters

These films, by their nature, will involve shoot-outs, bank heists, intra- and inter-gang warfare, prison escapes, electric chairs. These films are action films – dramatic things happen, often at immense speed. Some of these films go from one set piece to the next. There is an inbuilt thrust of the narrative as the hero is pursued either by the law or by other gangsters, and he rarely has time on his side.

The characters are larger than life. The conflicts they face may have their origin in everyday life, but they are so much bigger. The characters' strength to stand up to this way of life and all of its precarious aspects is an intriguing part of the film. They are frequently highly intelligent, wisecracking entertainers, as well as snappy dressers.

Combine these aspects of the gangster archetype and we have the source of many audience pleasures, especially those concerning the major and minor enigmas of the film:

- ■ Will he get away with it?
- ■ What will he do next?
- ■ How will he take control?
- ■ Will he face the electric chair?
- ■ Will we lose sympathy for him?
- ■ Do we want him to get caught?
- ■ Is it true?

over two dozen people killed on screen

In *The Godfather* we can see that there are many aspects of these conventions used. The narrative is packed full of action, with over two dozen people being killed on screen. There are numerous set pieces and dramatic moments, for example:

■ The wedding
■ The interviews with Don Corleone
■ The horse's head sequence
■ The attempted assassination of the Don
■ The murder of Sollozzo
■ The Sicily sequence: wooing, wedding and assassination
■ Sonny's attack on Carlo
■ The assassination of Sonny
■ The meeting of the dons
■ The Las Vegas sequence
■ The baptism sequence
■ The murder of the dons
■ Michael's crowning as the new don

There is never a dull moment in this film. Coppola manages to get the rhythm of the piece balanced. We have many quiet moments to reflect upon what is happening and to prepare us for the next dramatic key scene.

Where Coppola takes the genre to new levels, however, is in his very clear vision of the film being about the family and maintaining its metaphorical parallels with corporate America. The success of the film with an audience depends upon us seeing distinct groups of people:

■ The 'good' bad-guys – the Corleone family
■ The 'bad' bad-guys – the other families and Sollozzo
■ The law – who are corrupt

production history

Within what McKee calls 'a little world' (the essential dimension of any film narrative) Coppola makes us sympathise with the Corleone family all the way and, in particular, with the development of Michael. It is a film in which the hero succeeds in getting what he wants but at immense cost to himself. The arc of the film depends on this one honest, decent character who is brought into the evil world of his family because of filial love. The audience is let off the hook: we see Michael as having tragic proportions and the film works on this level emotionally. We feel sorry for him, for what he has become. Because his enemy is our enemy we do not feel intense regret at the many murders he is responsible for – they are all utterly reprehensible characters.

The other fundamental aspect of *The Godfather* generically is that no other film previously created such a convincing 'real' world of the Mafia family and much of the success of this is down to the **style** of the film and the detail of the narrative. The use of rites of passage and of daily rituals is very important here: we recognise this in our own lives. The way in which the family stick up for each other, love and destroy each other is an important part of the hook of the film.

production history

The Godfather had a very difficult birth. It began when a minor Italian-American writer decided that the worthy novels he was writing were receiving good reviews but were not paying the bills. He turned his hand to a form of fiction that was much derided in critical circles but was popular with audiences. The potboiler was dependent upon lively **narratives**, strong characters, plenty of sex and violence and a simple delivery. The idea came to Mario Puzo that he should set this novel in the world of the Mafia – something that had never been done as explicitly as he intended it to be. The working title for the novel was *Mafia*.

At the same time a young movie executive named Robert Evans had taken a major role in Paramount following the success of his film *Love Story* (1970). Evans was a very ambitious former actor and playboy, who intended his career shift to production to make him one of the leading players in the cut-throat business of Hollywood. When he realised that

an artist, not an artisan

Puzo, a gambler like himself, was in need of money to pay his debts while he was finishing the novel, Evans obtained the rights for the film option for $12,000 – one of the biggest steals in movie history.

The film eventually made it to a green light after Evans nearly lost the project to Burt Lancaster. The first problem was finding a director. The film was offered to countless directors, none of whom were interested as the project seemed to be cheap and sensationalist, and was a poor **representation** of Italians. The added problem from a production point of view was that a film called *The Brotherhood*, starring Kirk Douglas, bombed at the box office in 1968, at the end of a difficult decade for gangster films. The feeling was strong that the **genre** was tired and audiences were not interested in the Cosa Nostra. Evans stuck to his idea that the main reason these films failed was that they were dominated by Jewish producers/directors and what this film needed was a genuine Italian feel. So the search was on for an Italian director. The problem was, there weren't any established ones.

The only one available was Francis Ford Coppola (as he wished to be called at the time) who had three films to his name, none of which had made it at the box office. The only saving grace for Coppola was that he had just been nominated for an Oscar for his screenplay for *Patton* (1969). In desperation, Evans approached Coppola, but was immediately rejected. Coppola had high ambition, but he saw himself as an artist, not an artisan. His dream was to create a studio where he and other like-minded souls could produce their own films without the interference of Hollywood moguls, who were neither talented nor scrupulous. But the irony was, as his father pointed out, if this film made some money it would help to set this penniless director with a wife and two children (and another one on the way) on the path he wanted. Coppola reconsidered and accepted the offer from Evans.

Coppola and Evans had continual disagreements during the making of the film, right up to the final cut. To this day the argument continues as to who was responsible for this cut (see Style: The Director's Cut).

bibliography

general film

Altman, Rick, *Film Genre*, BFI, 1999
Detailed exploration of the concept of film genre

Arijon, Daniel, *Grammar of the Film Language*, Silman James Press, 1976
Clear visual illustrations of technique

Beaver, Frank, *Dictionary of Film Terms: The Aesthetic Companion to Film Analysis*, Twayne Publishers, 1994
Useful dictionary

Bordwell, David, *Narration in the Fiction Film*, Routledge, 1985
A detailed study of narrative theory and structures

– – –, Staiger, Janet & Thompson, Kristin, *The Classical Hollywood Cinema: Film Style & Mode of Production to 1960*, Routledge, 1985; pbk 1995
An authoritative study of cinema as institution, it covers film style and production

– – – & Thompson, Kristin, *Film Art*, McGraw-Hill, 4th edn, 1993
Informative and indispensable

Branson, Gill & Stafford, Roy, *The Media Student's Handbook*, Routledge, 2nd edn 1999

Buckland, Warren, *Teach Yourself Film Studies*, Hodder & Stoughton, 1998
Very accessible, it gives an overview of key areas in film studies

Cook, Pam & Bernink, Mieke (eds), *The Cinema Book*, BFI, 2nd edn 1999
Many aspects touched upon with numerous case studies

Corrigan, Tim, *A Short Guide To Writing About Film*, HarperCollins, 1994
Exactly that

Corrigan, Timothy, *A Cinema Without Walls: Movies and Culture After Vietnam*, Routledge, 1991
Very specific and puts modern American cinema into a political perspective

Dick, Bernard F., *Anatomy of Film*, St Martin's Press, 1998 (3rd edn)
A useful introduction

Dyer, Richard (with Paul McDonald), *Stars*, BFI, 2nd edn 1998
A good introduction to the star system

Easthope, Antony, *Classical Film Theory*, Longman, 1993
A clear overview of writing about film theory

Hayward, Susan, *Key Concepts in Cinema Studies*, Routledge, 1996
An academic dictionary

Hill, John & Gibson, Pamela Church (eds), *The Oxford Guide to Film Studies*, Oxford University Press, 1998
Comprehensively touches on many aspects

Hollows, Joanne & Jancovich, Mark, *Approaches to Popular Film*, Manchester University Press, 1995
A useful introduction

Jackson, Kevin, *The Language of Cinema*, Carcanet Press Limited, 1998
A useful dictionary, especially on technical terms

general film   bibliography

Kawin – Websites

Kawin, Bruce F., *How Movies Work*,
University of California Press, 1992
  An informative introduction

Lapsley, Robert & Westlake, Michael,
Film Theory: An Introduction,
Manchester University Press, 1994

Maltby, Richard & Craven, Ian,
Hollywood Cinema,
Blackwell, 1995
  A comprehensive work on the
  Hollywood industry and its
  products

McKee, Robert, *Story: Substance,
Structure, Style and the Principles of
Screenwriting*, Methuen, 1998
  A clear and direct analysis of story
  structure form the writer's point of
  view

Monaco, James, *How to Read a Film*,
Oxford University Press, 2000 (3rd edn)
  A useful introduction

Mottram, James, *Public Enemies: the
Gangster Movie A–Z*, BT Batsford, 1998
Indispensable if you love gangster films

Mulvey, Laura, 'Visual Pleasure and
Narrative Cinema' (1974), in *Visual
and Other Pleasures*,
Indiana University Press, Bloomington,
1989
  The classic analysis of 'the look' and
  'the male gaze' in Hollywood cinema.
  Also available in numerous other
  edited collections

Nelmes, Jill (ed.), *Introduction
to Film Studies*, Routledge, 2nd edn
1999
  Comprehensively covers most aspects

Nowell-Smith, Geoffrey (ed.),
The Oxford History of World Cinema,
Oxford University Press, 1996
  Hugely detailed and wide-ranging
  with many features on 'stars'

Thomson, David, *A Biographical
Dictionary of the Cinema*,
Secker & Warburg, 1975
  Unashamedly driven by personal taste,
  but often stimulating

Truffaut, François, *Hitchcock*, Simon &
Schuster, 1966, rev. edn. Touchstone,
1985
  Landmark extended interview

Turner, Graeme, *Film as Social Practice*,
3rd edn, Routledge, 1999
  Excellent introduction

Vogler, Christopher, *The Writer's
Journey: Mythic Structure for
Storytellers and Screenwriters*, Boxtree,
1996
  Understanding film as myth

Voytilla, Stuart, *Myth and the Movies:
Discovering the Mythic Structure of 50
Unforgettable Films*, Michael Wiese
Productions, 1999
  Applications of Vogler's ideas

Wollen, Peter, *Signs and Meaning in
the Cinema*, BFI 1997 (revised edn)
  An important study in semiology

Readers should also explore the many
relevant websites and journals.
Film Education and *Sight and Sound* are
standard reading.

Valuable websites include:

The Internet Movie Database at
www.uk.imdb.com

Screensite at
www.tcf.ua.edu/screensite/contents.html

The Media and Communications Site at
the University of Aberystwyth at
www.aber.ac.uk/~dgc/welcome.html

There are obviously many other
university and studio websites which are
worth exploring in relation to film
studies

THE GODFATHER

the godfather

Brown, Nick (ed.), *Francis Ford Coppola's The Godfather Trilogy*, Cambridge University Press, 2000
  Academic essays

Cowie, Peter, *The Godfather Book*, Faber & Faber, 1997
  A production history

Lebo, Harlan, *The Godfather Legacy*, Simon & Schuster, 1997
  A production history with useful stories

Puzo, Mario, *The Godfather* (novel), William Heinemann, 1969
  The original novel

Coppola

Bergan, Ronald, *Francis Coppola*, Orion Media, 1998
  A brief biography, concentrating on the films

Cowie, Peter, *Coppola*, Faber & Faber, 1989
  A detailed biography

Lewis, Jon, *Whom God Wishes to Destroy: Francis Coppola and the New Hollywood*, Athlone Press, 1995
  A biography that puts Coppola in the perspective of his time

Lourdeaux, Lee, *Italian and Irish Filmmakers in America: Ford, Capra, Coppola and Scorsese*, Temple University Press, 1990
  An academic text

Schumacher, Michael, *Francis Ford Coppola: a Filmmaker's Life*, Bloomsbury, 1999
  A detailed biography, packed with information

Brando

Brando, Marlon, *Brando: Songs My Mother Taught Me*, Century, 1994
  From the horse's mouth

Grobel, Lawrence, *Conversations with Brando*, Hyperion, 1991
  A long and fascinating interview with the star

McCann, Graham, *Rebel Males: Clift, Brando and Dean*, Hamish Hamilton, 1991
  Puts Brando into context, especially in relation to masculine representation

Schickel, Richard, *Brando: a Life in Our Times*, Pavilion Books, 1991
  A detailed biography

Tanitch, Robert, *Brando*, Random House, 1994
  A picture book with some comments

Hollywood

Biskind, Peter, *Easy Riders, Raging Bulls*, Bloomsbury, 1998
  Great gossip

Evans, Robert, *The Kid Stays in the Picture*, Aurum Press, 1994
  The brat himself speaks

Goldman, William, *Adventures in the Screen Trade*, Abacus, 1996
  One of the best introductions to working in Tinsel Town

Putnam, David, *Undeclared War*, HarperCollins, 1997
  An excellent history from a British perspective, from one who should know

Aristotle – Campbell

Other

Aristotle, *Poetics*
Where analysis began

Barthes, Roland, *S/Z*
Barthes' literary analysis of a Balzac
novel informs similar approaches in
film

**Campbell, Joseph, *The Hero with a
Thousand Faces*, Paladin, 1988**
The master explains the importance
of myths – the basis of Vogler's work

filmography

In addition to this filmography also consider other films referred to in this Note, especially those mentioned in Key Players' Biographies and Genre sections.

Apocalypse Now (Francis Ford Coppola, 1979)
One of Coppola's most ambitious films and greatest achievements. Must see

Bonnie and Clyde (Arthur Penn, 1967)
This film and *The Godfather* prevented the gangster genre from dying completely. The final death scenes in this film eerily prequel Sonny's demise

Bram Stoker's Dracula (Francis Ford Coppola, 1992)
Watch Coppola at his most flamboyant; he loves the melodrama

The Brotherhood (Martin Ritt, 1968)
This film was a flop and almost forced Paramount to give up on *The Godfather*. Same territory as the Coppola picture

Bugsy (Barry Levinson, 1991)
Another nostalgic gangster film

Casino (Martin Scorsese, 1995)
Another nostalgic gangster film

The Conversation (Francis Coppola, 1974)
An extraordinary and personal film for Coppola. This may show us the kind of film he would have continued to make if American Zoetrope had become the success that he dreamed of. A minor masterpiece

Donnie Brasco (Mike Newell, 1997)
Another nostalgic gangster film

The Freshman (Andrew Bergman, 1990)
A self-indulgent parody from Brando as Carmine Sabatini, and a send-up of *The Godfather* – great fun

The Godfather Part II (Francis Ford Coppola, 1974)
If ever there was a sequel that was better than the original, this is probably it. You cannot study *The Godfather* without seeing this film – a masterpiece

Godfather Part III (Francis Ford Coppola, 1990)
Coppola unrestrained in the most operatic and melodramatic film in the trilogy

Goodfellas (Martin Scorsese, 1990)
Another nostalgic gangster film

October (Eisenstein, 1928)
In 1959 Coppola saw Eisenstein's *October*. He later said, 'On Monday I was in the theatre, and on Tuesday I wanted to become a film-maker.' The impact on Coppola was intense to say the least: by the autumn of 1960 he had entered the UCLA Film School. Worth looking at to see where Coppola learnt to use montage

Once Upon a Time in America (Sergio Leone, 1984)
One of the greatest gangster films ever made, from the man who gave us spaghetti westerns. Epic, awe-inspiring – and not about Italians. De Niro shines

cinematic terms

The following terms are given very short definitions. Most of the important ones are elaborated at some point in the Note. These terms are mostly cinematic, but some are conceptual terms that can apply to many other areas.

allusion a reference to another person, place, event, work of art, literature, film, etc.

ambience the qualities of the natural environment

anti-climax the narrative denies the audience the high point they were expecting

archetype (usually) a basic character type that is seen as a template, e.g., the lover (Romeo)

auteur theory the concept that the director is the 'author' of the work

binary opposition conflicting aspects of the characters, themes or narratives of a film that help to provide structure

classical Hollywood style the style of editing, cinematography, etc., that was developed in the Hollywood Studio System, particularly during the period 1930–50

climax a highly dramatic point in a scene or film

close-up a shot that shows the whole face

closure the method used to end the film, usually with some finality

composition the arrangement of objects, characters, etc., in the frame

continuity editing a system of cutting the film together that retains clarity of action and narrative, usually with coherence of time and space

convention an accepted technique, style or aspect of structure that the audience readily accepts; established through time

counterpoint contrasting of two aspects at the same moment

crane shot one that moves up high and/or over some distance; the camera is on the end of a crane

cross-cutting cutting between two or more scenes quickly

cut a move to the next shot

dialogue the spoken words in the film, including accent, delivery, etc.

diegetic sound the sounds we hear in the world of the film (as contrasted with non-diegetic sound)

discourse the way in which a work of art reveals itself, e.g., in film, through sound, images, words and music

dissolve a fade-out of one scene as another fades in

dolly this shot involves the camera moving towards, or away from, the central action or object

ellipsis an edit that swiftly and cleverly jumps through time

enigma questions posed by the text to keep the audience interested, curious, tense, etc.

epic a narrative that covers years and is heroic in nature

extreme long shot this shot shows landscapes, streets, etc.

fade-in from a black screen gradually the picture appears on the screen

fade-out the picture on the screen gradually disappears, usually to black

foreshadow when an object, action, event, etc. hints at what is to occur in the narrative

frame an individual picture within a shot, or that which we can see in a frozen moment

genre a type or classification of film, e.g., the gangster film

hand-held shot a shot that follows a character, object, etc., with a slightly jittery effect as the camera is held in the hand of the camera operator

Hays code an ideological code of conduct set down by the Motion Picture Producers and Distributors of America in 1930 to control the moral, sexual and religious content of a film

hero the major character whom the audience sympathises with or relates to

high angle a shot from a high point looking down

ideology the ideas, beliefs and values that an individual, group or society holds to be true, valid or important

intertextuality the way in which one film text can refer to, or feed off, another

juxtaposition the effect created by placing two things next to each other, e.g., characters, objects, shots

long shot this shot shows whole figures in relation to their surroundings

low angle a shot taken by placing the camera below a character/action and looking up towards it

medium close-up a shot that is roughly from the mid-chest to the top of the head

medium long shot a shot that shows the whole body

medium shot a shot that is roughly from the knees upwards

Method acting a technique of acting developed from the work of the Russian director Konstantin Stanislavsky (1863–1938), involving realistic portrayals of character; it may include many aspects of characterisation to convince the audience of the reality of the scene

metonymy an object that represents something or someone it is closely related to

metteur-en-scène the person responsible for creating the film, usually the director

mise-en-scène composition and movement within a frame, including lighting, set, props, costumes; simply put, it is the world of the film that we see and hear

montage this term has many definitions, but it essentially involves the placing of images or scenes in a sequence; a form of editing

motif a recurrent idea, either visual or aural

narrative a chain of events in cause-effect relationships occurring in time and space

non-diegetic sound the sounds we hear that are not in the world of the film, such as the soundtrack and additional sound effects

non-verbal communication sometimes referred to loosely as body language, it involves all aspects of communication that are not relayed by the exact words themselves

cinematic terms

over-the-shoulder shot used mostly in shot/reverse shot, the camera is positioned just over the shoulder of an actor to give an impression of what they can see, especially who they are talking to or listening to

pan when the camera is moved, on a fixed pivot, to the right or the left

parallel narrative cutting together two narratives so that the audience can receive them more-or-less together

plot all the events that are directly presented to us in the film

point of view a shot that shows the point of view of a character; on a larger scale, a whole film may place one person's experiences as central

protagonist the leading character

reading the film text giving meaning to the film

realism the attempt to present the world of the film as truthful and realistic

representation the way individuals and groups are portrayed by the film

reverse zoom the lens makes the picture move further away from the action, usually in one continuous movement

schemata the mental models we have that enable us to understand a narrative

sequence a series of scenes

shot the one individual piece of film or even a single still

special effects effects achieved by unusual or technical means

spectacle a scene or film that is characterised by the grand, lavish or large scale

star a famous and popular actor who can sell a film

stereotype a means of labelling groups of people, or attributing particular qualities to them

style the way that the film is constructed; can reflect the way an individual director uses the script, etc.

sub-plot a minor plot within the overall narrative; can contrast with or parallel the main plot

subtext reading between the lines; what does the character really mean?

text the film itself

track the camera follows the action (the camera is on tracks for a smooth operation)

two-shot a shot that shows two people in it, usually talking to each other

willing suspension of disbelief the audience's collusion with the film-makers in pretending that the story is real

zoom a shot in which the lens makes the picture move closer to the action, usually in one continuous movement

credits

production company
Paramount Pictures

director
Francis Ford Coppola

producer
Albert S. Ruddy

screenplay
Mario Puzo and
Francis Ford Coppola

cast
Vito Corleone – Marlon Brando

Michael Corleone – Al Pacino

Sonny Corleone – James Caan

Peter Clemenza –
Richard Castellano

Tom Hagen – Robert Duvall

McCluskey – Sterling Hayden

Jack Woltz – John Marley

Barzini – Richard Conte

Kay Adams – Diane Keaton

Sollozzo – Al Lettieri

Fredo Corleone – John Cazale

Luca Brasi – Lenny Montana

Sal Tessio – Abe Vigoda

Appolonia – Simonetta Stefanelli